EXTRAORDINARY JEWS
Staging Their Lives

One-Act Plays for Teens

Gabrielle Suzanne Kaplan

A.R.E. Publishing, Inc.
Denver, Colorado

Acknowledgements

Grateful thanks to: Aaron Lansky and the people at the
National Yiddish Book Center; to all my students, who
were my "guinea pigs" as I was writing these plays; and
to Audrey Friedman Marcus and Rabbi Raymond A.
Zwerin of A.R.E. Publishing, Inc., my favorite editors and
publishers.

© A.R.E. Publishing, Inc. 2001

Published by:
Behrman House
Millburn, NJ

Library of Congress Control Number 2001089281
ISBN 978-0-86705-051-6

Printed in the United States of America
10   9   8   7   6   5   4   3   2

Dedication

This book is dedicated to all of the extraordinary
individuals I had the opportunity "to get to know" as I
researched and wrote about them. May each person who
reads this book be equally inspired.

Contents

Introduction

Today's Jewish teenagers need role models — individuals who have defied expectations, challenged society's beliefs, struggled hard with their own ambitions, and reached deep into their hearts and souls to create powerful, inspirational lives. The biographical plays in this book portray eight modern Jewish people — each of whom embodies the idea of *Tikkun Olam*, that we must all be in partnership with God to improve the world. These plays show that there is no single way to become a Jewish hero or heroine. Each of these individuals has a unique history, special talents, and has made difficult decisions.

By acting out these lives rather than just studying them, teenagers will have the opportunity to learn about these individuals from the inside out. Embodying a character teaches us things about a person that reading alone cannot. Drama can teach and inspire the actors and the audience, the stage crew and the director. Drama allows us to grow and learn in a community process.

The eight plays in this book are simple enough to be read in class, or they may be used for full productions with costumes, props, and sets. You might want to select a few of the plays to produce and create an evening of theater about the heroes of your choice. With a little guidance, teenagers can work together to stage these works. This book is also a worthwhile tool for research projects.

Bella Abzug: A Serious Woman

Characters

Bella Abzug
Radio Announcer
Martin Abzug
Esther, Bella's assistant
Various Congressmen
Reporter 1
Reporter 2
Reporter 3
Young Bella
Warden
Mother
Campaign Worker(s)

Setting

The play has several different settings; simple furniture
— tables and chairs — will work just fine. The play
begins in Bella's law office.

Props

Signs and banners, newspapers, and several telephones
are needed.

Costume

It is very important that Bella always wear the wide-
brimmed hats for which she was famous.

Scene 1

(It is 1970. Bella is in her office working late. She is listening to the radio as she works.)

Radio Announcer: The war in Vietnam continues to escalate. Civilian deaths increase every day. It does not appear that peace will come anytime soon.

(Bella stands up, turns off the radio and yells at it.)

Bella: And do you know why peace won't come anytime soon? It's because one half of the world's population has no power in decision making! There are no women in the peace talks, no women making international policy! Such an imbalance! How can one half of the world, the men only, make the decisions for all of us? It's simply not fair!

(Esther enters, interrupting her.)

Esther: Bella? Who were you talking to?

Bella: The world! The power structure! The powers that be!

Esther: I don't think they can hear you. We're on the 39th floor.

Bella: That won't stop me from yelling! I heard the news on the radio — you can't imagine how many civilians are dying.

Esther: I know. But you can't give up hope. There were so many demonstrators yesterday at the anti-war rally that you organized . . . so many young people.

Bella: I don't feel like I'm doing enough. Innocent people are dying. In Jewish scriptures we learn that we have a responsibility to heal the world . . .

Esther: You're one person, Bella. You're doing so much. (*Pause.*) And I'm just one person, too. I love being your assistant, but these late nights are killing me. It's almost eleven.

Bella: Go home, Esther. I'll make it up to you. Come in late tomorrow.

Esther: Thanks, Bella. You should go home, too. Get some rest.

Bella: I can't go home quite yet. I need to think some more. There's got to be something else I can do . . .

Esther: Good night, Bella.

(Esther exits. Bella paces the room.)

Bella: Let's see. I've been a civil rights lawyer for many years now. Back when I was in law school, there were only a few women law students in the whole country! I have a reputation — here in New York at least. And others are starting to take note. With my anti-Vietnam and anti-nuclear marches . . . humm, Bella Abzug . . . do I have enough name recognition . . . to be elected to office?

(The phone rings. Bella answers it. On the opposite side of the stage, Martin Abzug appears, holding a phone.)

Bella: Hello?

Martin: Bella, darling, what are you doing in your office? It's nearly midnight!

Bella: Martin, I lost track of time completely. I've been doing some serious thinking . . .

Martin: Bella, we've been married all these years, raised two beautiful daughters. I think I know you well enough to say . . . you are always doing some serious thinking!

Bella: This is different, Martin. I am thinking about something that . . . I've only dreamed of before.

Martin: Nu? Why don't you come home and tell me about it?

Bella: I can't wait that long to tell you! Martin, I've decided . . . to run for Congress!

Martin: Congress! My Bella? Congresswoman Abzug. That has a nice ring. When do we start campaigning?

Bella: Well, I suppose I have to file a petition . . . and get signatures . . . and make signs . . . and phone calls . . . and . . .

Martin: And write a platform. What will your platform be, Bella?

Bella: Peace for children and all living things. Equal opportunities for women and minorities. Getting women into positions of political power. After all, women belong in the House!

Martin: I like it!

Bella: Women belong in the House . . . and in the Senate, Martin.

Martin: If anyone can tell them that, it's my Bella.

Bella: I suppose I should come home and rest.

Martin: Come home, Bella. Tomorrow will be a big day.

Scene 2

(A press conference. Bella stands behind a podium, surrounded by reporters and onlookers. Esther and Martin are also there.)

Bella: And so, I announce my candidacy for Congresswoman. That has a nice ring, "Congresswoman." Are there any questions?

Reporter 1: There are currently only 11 women in Congress from the entire United States. What makes you think this country is ready for one more . . . especially a woman like you who is so . . . outspoken?

Bella: I do not believe that the test for whether or not you can hold a job should be the arrangement of your chromosomes, sir. And, in terms of my "outspokenness," let me tell you something. In Yiddish, we have a word called *chutzpah*. Do you know what *chutzpah* means?

Reporter 1: Uh, no, ma'am. No I don't.

Bella: Well, look at me. I may just be *chutzpah* personified! That means, I say what I need to say, and I don't care who I offend! And do you know why? Because the policies in this country offend me! Because I don't believe that our young men should be killed in Vietnam, and I don't believe in economic policies that keep people living in poverty. So I speak out! What would be better — to stand back and watch people die?

Reporter 2: Miss, uh, Mrs. . . . uh —

Bella: Ms.

Reporter 2: Ms. Abzug. You have certainly had a very interesting career as a civil rights lawyer. Yet, you have not always won your cases. I am thinking of the Willie McGee affair. How do we know you will be more successful as a Congresswoman?

Bella: I haven't always won my cases. But I have tried to fight against injustices. I can't promise you more than that.

Reporter 3: Tell us about the Willie McGee case. Weren't you defending a dangerous rapist?

Bella: Willie McGee. Let's set the record straight . . .

(Downstage or across from the press conference, a young Bella, very pregnant, and the Warden, appear. The focus shifts to them, as Bella sets the stage for their story.)

Bella: The year was 1949. Stories of a young black man accused of raping a white woman in Mississippi had reached us up North. Apparently, the two of them had been having an affair for three years, but now rape charges were being pressed. The man was going to be executed for his crime and couldn't get decent legal representation. There was clear racism at play. I knew I had to go help that man.

Reporter 3: But you were only 29 years old. And, you were seven months pregnant! And you went down South, alone?

(The press conference freezes. Young Bella speaks.)

Young Bella: Hello, you must be the Warden.

Warden: *(In a southern drawl.)* How can I help you ma'am? Please take a seat. I'm not used to seeing women in your . . . condition.

Young Bella: I'm just pregnant, Warden. Otherwise, I'm the picture of health! The baby's not due for another two months. Hopefully I can get my business finished way before then!

Warden: I can tell by your . . . your accent . . . that you don't come from Mississippi.

Young Bella: The Bronx. Born and bred. Now I live in Manhattan. You ever been to New York, Warden?

Warden: Can't say as I have.

Young Bella: Oh, you should come some time! I love New York! Where else in the entire world do you get such a mix of people? Chinese, Japanese, Jewish, Italian — and the food is incredible! Culture? Have we got culture! The Black jazz musicians, the —

Warden: How exactly can I help you, ma'am?

Young Bella: I am Bella Abzug, I just got off the train from New York City. I'm here to meet with my client, Willie McGee, before the trial.

Warden: You are Bella Abzug!

Young Bella: The one! You've heard of me down here?

Warden: Oh, we know who you are, all right. The Jackson newspapers have been writing about you.

Young Bella: I know the case has received a lot of press coverage. It seems people love reading about executions. Brutal.

Warden: They ain't just writing about the execution of Willie McGee. They're writing about you — the Jewish woman lawyer from New York.

Young Bella: Well, I am Jewish. I'm a woman. And I'm from New York. At least they have their facts straight.

Warden: Yes, ma'am. They're calling to "lynch that Jewish woman lawyer!"

Young Bella: Lynch! The newspapers wrote that?

Warden: I'm afraid so. (*Pause.*) So, if I was you, I'd forget this whole affair — especially in your condition. Get back on the train and go home to New York. I'm sure your family misses you.

Young Bella: And I miss them. But I have a job to do here. A clear injustice is going on. In the United States of America, everyone has the right to an attorney and to a fair trial.

Warden: Have you made a hotel reservation?

Young Bella: Excuse me?

Warden: A hotel . . . to stay in while you're here. The trial could drag on for quite some time.

Young Bella: I want to meet with my client first. Then I'll take care of my lodging. I imagine there are plenty of hotels in a city like Jackson.

Warden: Yes, there are quite a few.

Young Bella: Very good. Now, if you can . . .

Warden: Yup, there's lotsa hotels in Jackson. But ain't none of 'em will rent a room to you. That was in the paper as well. They joined together and made a decision. Said no woman Jewish lawyer could stay at their place! (*Pause.*) So, like I said, I could give you a ride back to the train station and you could get yourself back to New York . . .

Young Bella: There's one thing you'll discover about me, Warden. I am a very serious woman. I didn't leave my family and take a train to the Deep South just to turn around and go home because some overgrown bullies have nothing better to do than to try and scare little ol' me. Well, it's not so easy to scare Bella Abzug, and if they don't know that now, they'll have to find out the hard way! I'm staying put until Willie McGee gets a fair trial with a decent lawyer — me! Now, take me to my client, Warden. We've wasted enough time with this small talk.

Warden: Yes, ma'am. Right this way.

(*They exit, and focus returns to the press conference.*)

Bella: You're right. I didn't win that case. It was a tragedy and remains a tragedy for this country that Willie McGee was executed. But I fought my hardest to defend

9

his freedom. The day the trial was over, I slept sitting up in the bus station. But my desire to fight against injustice . . . I learned as a little girl when my Grandfather took me to synagogue. That's what being Jewish means — to work to repair the world. That is exactly what I would do as a Congresswoman.

Reporter 1: Ms. Abzug, it seems you have often defended the underdog of American society. Tell us about your involvement in Senator Joseph McCarthy's search for un-American activities . . .

Bella: Joe McCarthy? That wasn't a search! That was a witch-hunt!

Reporter 3: Are you convinced that none of the clients you defended were Communists?

Bella: Communists? The people under attack by Joe McCarthy were artists, thinkers, writers . . . people whose lives were wrecked by Joe McCarthy. I was able to defend a few of them . . .

(Young Bella and her client enter the opposite side of the stage. The press conference freezes again.)

Client: Someone informed on me! I can't imagine who it could have been? What is my crime, Bella? I've always belonged to political groups. I thought we had the right to free speech in America. I express my views. I'm not trying to overthrow the government.

Young Bella: These are dangerous times in America. Who would think that in the 1950s after we've won World War II, we'd have such a witch-hunt going on . . . right in our own country?

Client: I'm not a Communist. I may be left wing, but since when is that a crime? I have never even talked to a member of the Communist party!

Young Bella: Senator McCarthy is the one who is un-American. Trust me. That is what history will show.

Client: History may show that, but I'm worried now . . . about the present. I don't want to go to jail. I don't want to lose my job. It's starting to happen in Hollywood. Famous actors are getting blacklisted. You know about that, Bella. So many actors and writers, directors, musicians — they can't get work. No one will hire them. Once you're on McCarthy's list, you're cursed. How will I support my family if I lose my job?

Young Bella: This clown has no case against you! There's no way he can win. I don't care if we have to work day and night until your court hearing, we will build a case they can't refute. America's values are on the line here. We can't let Joe McCarthy ruin our country with his paranoia and suspicion. America is better than that.

Client: Thank you for being on my side, Bella. Thank you.

Young Bella: Esther! Esther! We need some coffee! It's going to be a late night!

(Young Bella and Client exit.)

Reporter 2: So you had more success with those hearings. And no one can dispute that you're a hard worker. But in the end, why should we give you our vote for Congress?

Bella: Young man, I began speaking my mind when I was just a girl. At 12 years old, I would ride the New York subway cars, giving speeches for the Zionist movement. When I was 13 years old, my beloved father died. I went into an Orthodox synaogogue and insisted on saying *Kaddish*, the prayer for our departed. And I said it in that very synagogue, where women were not allowed to do such a thing. The Creator gives us all many gifts. It seems that I have been blessed with the courage to speak out and defend what is right. In our country right now, there are many injustices. Poverty. Racism. The war in Vietnam. Damage to our environment. Sexism. If you elect me — Bella Abzug — I will go to Congress and I will speak out!

(Everyone at the press conference cheers loudly.)

Reporter 1: You've got to admit . . . the lady does have *chutzpah*!

Scene 3

(Back in Bella's office, which is now her campaign headquarters. Five or more telephones are placed around the room. Signs, banners, etc., are all around. Bella, Bella's Mother, and Martin are each talking on one of the phones. Esther and several campaign workers are typing, licking envelopes, or are engaged in another task.)

Radio Announcer: Tension is mounting on college campuses across the country as students continue to protest the war in Vietnam. President Nixon shows no intention of withdrawing our troops . . .

Bella: Shut that damned thing off! I can't hear myself think!

12

Esther: No, I'm sorry . . . no, she can't come then, she has another interview.

Bella: Esther, I'll be there, whatever it is, I'll be there! Sorry, as I was saying, the war in Vietnam is not moral in any . . .

Esther: I'm sorry, just a minute. Bella you can't be there, you have another interview scheduled at that time . . .

Mother: She's on another call right now. But I can talk to you. I'm her Mother!

Bella: Hold on! Esther, I'll be there! As I was saying . . .

Mother: To be honest, I don't know how come the war in Vietnam is still going on. My Bella has been protesting it for such a long time!

Esther: Just a moment, sir. Bella, you can't be two places at once!

Bella: I strongly disagree with Mr. Nixon. Esther, who says I can't be in two places at once! I'm Bella Abzug. I'll find a way!

Esther: She will be there, sir. I imagine she may be just a tad late.

Martin: Esther, look at these campaign brochures I've had printed. I'm going to go door-to-door!

Esther: You're what?

Martin: Door-to-door, like in the old days. I'll say, "Vote for my wife — she's the greatest!"

Esther: We really need to have a strategy meeting.

Bella: If I am elected, I will make a motion on my very first day in Congress to withdraw troops. You bet.

Mother: Hold on. What'd you say, Bella? You'll do what, darlink?

Bella: Mama, I'll make a motion in Congress to pull troops out of Vietnam!

Mother: Well, you should hear. She has big plans!

Bella: What? Oh yes, my mother's here. She's part of my campaign team. Yes, I've learned an awful lot from my mother. She came to this country from Russia, and she raised us kids alone after my father died.

Mother: Bella, shh! Don't tell them such things.

Bella: Why, Mama, I'm proud! Now is that enough for your article?

Mother: You should hear — such a daughter! Like no one ever saw.

Esther: Bella, should your mother be taking calls?

(A campaign worker enters with an armful of newspapers.)

Worker: Well, you've caused quite a storm, Bella! You should hear what the papers are calling you! Look at this headline, "Hurricane Bella!"

Martin: Hurricane Bella! I like that!

Mother: Is it a compliment?

Worker: There's more — "Mother Courage," for instance.

Mother: Now *that* I like!

Esther: Do you have all the papers — the front page, the editorials?

Worker: Yup, I've got them all.

Bella: Nu? So, what are they writing?

Worker: You've certainly caused a . . . reaction. The press isn't used to someone who speaks up like you do! Especially . . . a woman!

Martin: That's my Bella.

Esther: So the press was positive?

Worker: There is some concern . . . about Hurricane Bella actually getting elected seeing as how there are only 11 women in Congress from the entire country.

Bella: So, we need more!

Worker: You're the only one running on women's rights and a peace platform. It's pretty unusual.

Martin: So the American people want their sons to keep dying? They don't want their wives and sisters and mothers to have a say in anything?

Worker: It's not just that, it's . . . well, this paper points out . . . Bella is Jewish . . . and a woman. I mean, there are few women in Congress. And there are a few Jews in Congress. But there are no Jewish women Congressmen.

I mean Congresswomen. Bella would have to break down a lot of walls. Are New Yorkers ready for that?

Bella: There's only one way to find out. I'll have to go out there and talk to New Yorkers.

Esther: You can't just go out there! We need strategy, a plan . . .

Martin: I'll go door-to-door.

Mother: Me, too!

Bella: I'll take my mandolin and I'll sing! People love that!

Esther: Am I in an insane asylum? We are running a political campaign, not a talent show!

Worker: This paper points out the diversity of the constituents in the district where you're running. Jewish people might elect a Jewish woman, but there are lots of different groups here – I'm talking Chinatown, Little Italy!

Bella: People are people! I believe that everyone on the planet wants peace. People want justice for women and minorities . . . and for anyone treated unfairly. The people will elect me. Just wait and see!

Esther: Could we please talk strategy now?

Bella: Esther, take a break. Go home.

Martin: I'm hungry. Let's order Chinese! I'll give the delivery boy your new brochures!

Mother: Oh, let's see them, Martin.

Martin: "Bella Abzug for Congress! Because women belong in the House — the House of Representatives!"

Bella: *L'chaim!*

Everyone: *L'chaim!*

Scene 4

(At the polls. Only Bella is onstage, carrying a large campaign sign. Voice of the Radio Announcer is heard.)

Radio Announcer: Yes, ladies and gentlemen, be sure to get to those voting booths. You only have an hour left. In New York City's 19th district, the race is tight, with "Hurricane" Bella Abzug challenging Republican Barry Farber. The city of New York and the rest of the nation are waiting to see the outcome of this most unusual race!

Bella: How are you tonight, sir? Madam? Good to meet you. Yes, I am the one, I am Bella Abzug! You like my hat? Well, thank you! Yes, ma'am, I promise to help Chinatown . . . to help the entire 19th district . . . and the whole country, if I can! How? I will demand we pull troops out of Vietnam! I will demand we protect our environment! I will demand that women have equal rights. That's right — equal rights for everyone! The Torah, our Jewish sacred text, says "Justice, justice shall you pursue!" I take those words very seriously! I am a very serious woman.

(Lights fade.)

Scene 5

(Back at Bella's office. Martin, Esther, Mother, and campaign workers are waiting for Bella and for the election results.)

Martin: Where is she? The polls have been closed for some time now. We agreed to meet back here after the polls closed.

Mother: She can't stop, my Bella. She'll fight till the end!

Esther: Turn up the radio! The results should be in any minute!

Worker: Should I go out and look for her?

Martin: Let's get ready to pop the champagne . . .

Esther: Martin, please. You know as well as I do how close this race could be. I don't know if the people of New York are ready to elect a Jewish woman who is for peace.

Mother: But it's Bella. Of course they'll elect her.

Worker: Everybody . . . wait . . . listen . . .

Radio Announcer: And in the 19th district . . . there is a new representative to Congress —

(Bella enters.)

Radio Announcer: Ms. Bella Abzug!

Everyone: (All cheer.) Bella! Wow! *Mazal tov*! Congratulations! (etc.)

Bella: What, you were worried I wouldn't win?

Mother: I never doubted you.

Martin: Let's celebrate!

Bella: First, I want to thank each and every one of you, for working so hard and sacrificing so much for this campaign. Thanks to my devoted Mother, to the love of my life, Martin, to our beautiful daughters, to all of you fantastic volunteers, and to my dedicated assistant, Esther.

Esther: It has certainly been . . . like no other experience in my life.

Bella: Thank you.

Martin: Now, let's celebrate!

Bella: Tonight, we celebrate! Tomorrow, I start working!

Mother: So soon? Relax a little.

Bella: There is so much work to be done, Mother, so many wrongs to right. People are counting on me.

Mother: You've never let us down, Bella. Never.

Bella: And where do you think I learned to be so tough and to work so hard?

Mother: *(Laughing.)* I can't imagine!

Bella: From my Mother.

(They embrace.)

Martin: A toast! To the most outstanding member of Congress I've ever seen, my wife, Bella Abzug!

Everyone: To Bella!

(Lights down.)

Scene 6

(Bella's first day in Congress.)

Congressman 1: Well, here she is . . . the new Congresswoman from New York — Hurricane Bella!

Bella: That's what they call me.

Congressman 2: Now that you're in Congress, Bella, you'll grow to understand that the government moves at a slow pace. The radical ideas you campaigned on don't have a place here. Change is slow, and with President Nixon in office, the country is turning more conservative again.

Bella: The government may be slow, but not Bella Abzug! It looks like our session is starting. Excuse me. I'll take my seat.

(She does so.)

House Speaker: Welcome to our new session in Congress. We will begin this session by looking at any new resolutions.

Bella: (*Standing.*) Mr. Speaker, sir, this is my very first day in Congress. I propose a resolution that is so urgent, I feel

I must speak up! I call for the withdrawal of all troops from Indochina by July 4th of this year!

House Speaker: Did I hear you correctly? By July 4th?

Bella: Yes, Mr. Speaker.

Congressman 1: But that's only a few months away!

Congressman 2: Looks like a hurricane has just hit Congress!

Bella: Our young men are dying. Vietnamese civilians are dying. This is a very serious matter, my fellow Congressmen and Congresswomen. I am not afraid to work on serious issues. As you will find out, I may be funny, crass, loud, full of *chutzpah*, but there is one thing about Bella Abzug you can't deny — I am a very serious woman!

Bella Abzug, also known as "Hurricane Bella" and "Battling Bella," served as a Congresswoman from 1971 to 1977. She fought tirelessly for an end to the Vietnam War, and in support of such causes as reproductive freedom and gay rights. She helped found several liberal political organizations, among them the National Women's Political Caucus, which aimed at increasing the participation of women in government. In 1976, Ms. Abzug relinquished her seat in Congress and ran for the U.S. Senate; she was defeated by Daniel P. Moynihan. Despite this loss, she continued to play a major role in advocacy. She headed the Women's Environment and Development Organization, which worked to help improve the environment. She is remembered for her fighting spirit, and for her legacy of working for civil rights, women's rights, and peace and equality for all. She died in 1998 at age 78.

Leonard Bernstein: A Jewish American Genius

Characters*

Leonard Bernstein
Young Leonard
Mother
Father
Aaron Copland
Curtis students
Madame Helga
Ballet students
Arthur Rodzinski
Bruno Walter
Fans
Reporters
Felicia Bernstein
Jamie Bernstein
Alexander Bernstein
Nina Bernstein

*Several actors can play multiple roles if necessary.

Setting

The goal of the play is to imagine Leonard Bernstein on the concert stage. The characters that come out onto stage for scenes are part of his memory. Therefore, no actual set is needed: just Bernstein, center stage, ready to conduct.

Costumes

Ideally, Bernstein will be dressed for conducting in a tuxedo or fancy suit. The other characters can wear plain clothes.

Sound Design

Music is a critical part of conveying Leonard Bernstein's life. Efforts should be made to find and use the suggested recordings.

(Leonard Bernstein walks onto stage. He stands center stage, back to audience, with a baton in his right hand. He raises his arms as if to start conducting. He stops, turns, and gazes out at the audience. He relaxes his arms and addresses them, casually.)

Leonard: Can you imagine what it's like in that moment — that utterly quiet moment, just before the conductor is swept up in an ocean of sound? There is nothing like it in the world. I have no words to describe it. First, there is silence. Nothing. Then, with the wave of the arms, there is music. Wave after wave of music washes over me, carrying me up and over them. It is a mystery — no matter how we study or try to explain it — music is mystery. I remember the first time I conducted the New York Philharmonic. I was just 25 years old. This was highly unusual . . . unheard of. The year was 1943. Conductors were dusty old European men, not young Americans. Young Jewish Americans. I shocked the entire world! As a child, I didn't dream of being a conductor. I didn't really know what music was all about then. No one taught me. My father was a religious man. What mattered to him was studying the Talmud. Music was not taken seriously.

(Young Leonard and his Father enter. Leonard watches them with interest.)

Father: So you see, Moshe Rabaynu, our wise ancestor, teaches us many things. Leonard! Leonard, are you paying attention to me?

Young Leonard: Yes — Yes, Papa.

Father: And I was saying?

Young Leonard: Moshe Rabaynu, our wise ancestor, teaches us many things.

Father: You were listening! I'm mistaken. I thought I — I heard a faint humming. Were you humming to yourself, Leonard, while I was teaching you?

Young Leonard: I guess I was.

Father: And what exactly were you humming?

Young Leonard: "Barney Google."

Father: "Barney Google?"

Young Leonard: It's a popular song. "Barney Google, with the goo-goo-googly eyes."

Father: What nonsense! How can you fill your head with such nonsense?

Young Leonard: I like it, Papa. I like popular songs. Ragtime.

Father: Leonard, you're not like the other boys at the Boston Latin School. You have a destiny to fulfill. To become a great Rabbi, just like your grandfather. He was one of the most respected Hasidic Rabbis in Europe. You are a bright boy, Leonard, you learn very quickly. But you can't become a great Jewish leader by thinking about Barney Google.

Young Leonard: Can we finish for today, Papa?

Father: You need to learn discipline, Leonard. Great thinkers need a disciplined mind. We'll continue with the text.

Young Leonard: Rabba said, Moshe Rabaynu teaches us three things . . .

(Leonard starts to speak. The other characters quietly exit.)

Leonard: Even before I knew music, I was drawn to it. I couldn't imagine being a Rabbi, the life my father wanted for me. But the discipline he gave me through our study — that has helped me all through my lifetime. I could not have composed all that I have — orchestral works, operas, musicals, movie scores, chamber music — without discipline. (*Pause.*) When I was ten years old, my life changed. In one of those truly magnificent strokes of luck, my Aunt Rose needed to get rid of her piano.

(Leonard's Mother and Father enter the stage.)

Mother: Your sister Rose stopped by today. She's moving into a smaller apartment and has to get rid of a few things.

Father: Rose moving again? What does she want to get rid of this time?

Mother: She is kind to offer us these things. She can give us a few chairs, which we desperately need for when the whole family comes for *Seder*. Oh, and she can also give us her piano.

Father: Piano? What would we want with that? Why did Rose spend her good money on that thing anyway?

Mother: You know how she tends to be extravagant. I think it would be nice to have a piano. Our parlor is so dark and empty. I could put flowers on it. When company comes, I could put out little bowls of nuts on the piano. That would be nice.

Father: Well, if you think you could use it, let's take it. I suppose Rose would be heart-broken if the piano didn't at least stay in the family.

(They exit.)

Leonard: It never occurred to them that I might be interested in a piano. They certainly weren't about to spend money for me to take piano lessons. But once those beautiful keys were sitting there in our apartment, I couldn't stay away!

(Music from offstage: a child starting to bang on piano keys. The voices are heard from offstage, as Leonard listens, amused.)

Mother: Leonard! Stop that banging!

Father: Go to bed! We're trying to sleep!

Young Leonard: I can't sleep, Papa! I want to play!

Mother: You're not playing! You're banging! Enough!

Young Leonard: I'm learning to play, Mama! Soon I'll be able to play concertos and . . .

Mother: Such a dreamer, this boy!

Father: Leonard, that's all for tonight. We need to sleep.

Young Leonard: Oh, all right. Good night.

Leonard: As soon as I got home from school, I would immediately finish my homework and then start banging on the keys. Soon, I was playing simple songs — tunes I heard on the radio — and then I began to master pieces that were more complex.

(Music: a Mozart piano concerto. Again, the voices are heard from offstage.)

Mother: Leonard, stop banging! We need our sleep!

Father: You stop now, Leonard, or tomorrow I'll throw that piano out the window!

Young Leonard: But, listen — I'm finally learning Mozart.

Mother: Mozart, Shmozart — people need their rest!

Young Leonard: Okay, I'll stop for tonight.

Mother: It's beautiful when you play, Leonard, but not at one in the morning when normal people are sleeping. You understand me, darling?

Young Leonard: I didn't realize it was so late. I'm sorry. Good night, Mom. Good night, Dad.

Father: He didn't realize? Oy. The boy — he gets lost in music. When he plays, it's as if he drifts off into his own world.

Leonard: My father was right. When I listened to music, especially when I played music, I did enter another world — one in which an artist strives for perfection. In which an artist struggles, struggles . . . to create something eternal in time. (*Pause.*) I liked all kinds of music. I loved

28

classical music, but I still liked the Barney Google stuff, popular music, show tunes, jazz. As a teenager, I discarded my father's dream that I become a Rabbi. I applied to Harvard University and was accepted. I loved my studies there — literature, philosophy, science . . . and music. At Harvard, I met great thinkers and artists. When I was 19 years old, I met a man who would change my life — Aaron Copland.

(Aaron Copland enters. Young Leonard enters after him, knocks at his study door.)

Copland: Yes?

Young Leonard: Hello . . . Mr. Copland?

Copland: Can I help you?

Young Leonard: I know you've come to Harvard for only a brief visit, sir, and you must have a full schedule, but if I could take only a few minutes of your time, I was wondering if I could talk with you . . .

Copland: I like your courage and style. Very few undergraduates would have the nerve to come unannounced and knock at my door.

Young Leonard: I conducted one of your pieces for the chamber orchestra here last semester. I really enjoy conducting your music! I can't believe I'm standing here talking to the greatest living American composer.

Copland: So you're interested in conducting? That's very good. This country needs strong, vibrant conductors. American musicians seem to have an inferiority complex — as if only Europeans are distinguished enough to conduct.

Young Leonard: I love American music. In the pieces I compose, I use distinctly American sounds, just as you do.

Copland: You conduct, and you compose! Let me hear a little something or I'll think you're a phony baloney who walked in here for some fraternity prank.

Young Leonard: Yes, sir, you'll find I am very serious about my music. I would be honored to play for you.

Copland: Come then, sit down. Play!

(From offstage, Aaron Copland's "Piano Concerto" plays for a few moments. Copland and Young Leonard exit.)

Leonard: Imagine! I'm a teenage kid from Lawrence, Massachusetts, playing an Aaron Copland piece . . . for Aaron Copland! Fortunately, he liked my playing. He even made a special trip back to Harvard to hear the debut of a chamber piece I composed. Aaron Copland guided me to the Curtis Institute of Music in Philadelphia, where I studied . . . conducting with Fritz Reiner. (*Pause.*) I loved studying at Curtis . . . though the other students didn't always love having me there.

(Curtis students enter.)

Student 1: Did you hear Bernstein in class today? I could slug that egghead!

Student 2: That "Hah-vahd" boy . . . always bringing up philosophy and art and blah blah blah! I wish he'd shut up. This is a music school! We're here to study music.

Student 3: And the profs just eat it up! Did you hear Reiner today? "Please, go on Leonard . . ."

Student 1: Maybe we should think of ways to make our little genius's life really fun!

Student 2: He already has no social life, gets no party invitations. What else can we do?

Student 3: Such a smart guy must already know we don't like him.

Student 1: Tell you what guys. Smartie-pants might be a hit at Curtis, but he'll never make it in the real world. Can you imagine any orchestra putting up with the way he drones on?

Student 2: You're right! Just think of it! That'll be our revenge. Leonard Bernstein won't make it as a conductor! I bet he'll end up playing piano in some second-rate bar.

Student 3: And his compositions, too — terrible! He thinks he's a composer! You know, we should feel sorry for the guy.

Student 1: Leonard Bernstein: An American failure!

(They laugh, making remarks about Bernstein as they exit.)

Leonard: Those students had no education besides music. I looked at the world differently. I could not imagine music as an island unto itself. I understood language and science and art and music to be intimately connected. (*Pause.*) Aside from those students, my years at Curtis were fantastic. I was making great connections in the music world through my professors. When I finished my studies, I had many good recommendations, and hoped to find a job as an assistant conductor. Unfortunately, in 1942, no positions were open. So I moved to New York City and worked as an accompanist for dance classes.

(Young Leonard enters and sits at chair, as if he were at a piano, on one side of the stage. On the other side, Madame Helga and dancers enter.)

Madame Helga: Ladies, ladies. What a sloppy crew! Heads high, stomachs in! That's it — that's it! Now when I say pli-é, I mean pli-é! Mr. Bernstein, if you'd be so kind — and a-one, and a-two . . .

(Music: Simple ballet accompaniment.)

Madame Helga: Up and down, and back and forth. Up and down and back and forth. Very nice, Miss Jane. Back and forth! Miss Anna, you look like a swine — hold your stomach in! Back and forth, up and down — listen to the tempo, up and down. Ahh, Mr. Bernstein, your playing is beautiful. Miss Helen, you've lost your form entirely! And up and down and one and two . . .

(Music fades and they exit.)

Leonard: All of my studies . . . and for what? To spend my life in a cramped little dance studio listening to that incessant droning? *(Pause.)* But life is strange and mysterious, and our fates often take dramatic turns. On August 25, 1943, on my 25th birthday, I was called to the office of Arthur Rodzinski, conductor of the New York Philharmonic Orchestra.

(Rodzinski enters. Young Leonard enters next, approaches him.)

Rodzinski: Leonard Bernstein?

Young Leonard: Mr. Rodzinski?

Rodzinski: Leonard Bernstein, I have heard many great things about you from your professors at the Curtis Institute. You have made quite an impression at your young age. How old are you?

Young Leonard: Today is my birthday. I'm 25.

Rodzinski: Twenty-five! A child. (*Pause.*) How do you earn a living, Mr. Bernstein? A struggling, 25-year-old composer needs bread, too.

Young Leonard: I work for several ballet studios. At least I get to practice my playing.

Rodzinski: Ah, yes. I remember many years spent playing for ballet classes. The constant pounding of the stick, the ballet master's annoying drone. Tell me, Mr. Bernstein, are you seeking other employment?

Young Leonard: I'm seeking any work that will help me get closer to my dream of becoming a conductor.

Rodzinski: Do you know much about the life of an assistant conductor — say, an assistant here at the New York Philharmonic? You see, an assistant conductor must attend each and every rehearsal. He must study the scores and be prepared to go on at a moment's notice. He must be willing to do whatever the conductor asks of him. He is paid very little, but he gets to work very hard. The assistant lives here at Carnegie Hall because he must always be available. The truth of the matter is, the assistant conductor will almost never go onstage. He works for little glory.

Young Leonard: I'll do it! I'll do it! That is, if you're offering me the job.

Rodzinski: I've heard about your enthusiasm. Yes, I'd like you to become our assistant conductor.

Young Leonard: Thank you, Mr. Rodzinski. I can start immediately. Whenever you need me. Today. (*Pause.*) May I ask, Mr. Rodzinski, how did you choose me for this position? I mean, choose me from among all my classmates at Curtis?

Rodzinksi: I am a religious man, which you'll come to understand. God speaks to me in my prayers. God led me to hire you.

(They are both silent for a moment.)

Rodzinski: Who among us can understand our purpose in the universe? Why is one man destined for greatness while another is not?

Young Leonard: Thank you, Mr. Rodzinksi. I will try my hardest to show you that you made the right choice.

(They shake hands and exit.)

Leonard: So at 25, I became the youngest assistant conductor in the history of the New York Philharmonic Orchestra . . . and all because of Arthur Rodzinski's prayers. He was right about the work. It was grueling. Rehearsals were endless. Late into the night, I would stay up playing piano, just as I'd done when I was a boy. I was compelled to work on my own compositions, even as I was learning the works of the great masters. I wanted to conduct, to compose, to teach, to learn. My life was exhausting, but fulfilling. Then one day, everything changed . . .

(In this next scene, characters may speak directly to the audience. Rodzinski enters.)

Rodzinkski: It was Sunday afternoon, November 13, 1943. I was hours away from New York City, at my farm in Stockbridge. After all, the conductor of one of the world's most important orchestras needs some time to relax, too! I was not worried about the Philharmonic at all. *(Motions toward Bruno Walter who enters.)* The very distinguished Bruno Walter was with them, serving as guest conductor. And of course, Leonard was around. Not that we'd need him. But just in case.

Walter: It had been a busy week. The particular musical selections for the afternoon concert were very challenging. Strauss's "Don Quixote," a piece by Wagner, one by Schumann, and a new composition by Miklos Rosza called "Theme and Variations." We had been working hard all week to prepare. During the Saturday evening performance, I began to feel tired, weak, not quite myself. But I kept going.

Rodzinski: A conductor of a major philharmonic orchestra calling in sick? Impossible! I can't recall ever hearing of such a thing.

Walter: Sunday morning, I woke with fever, chills, and aches. A doctor was called to my hotel room. I was very, very ill. My wife called the manager of the Philharmonic. Tell him to call Lenny, I told her. Lenny Bernstein. He's got to step in for me.

Bernstein: The night before, I'd stayed out until almost sunrise. It was the debut of one of my new compositions, at a small cabaret, but an important step for me, nonetheless. My parents had come down from Boston for the occasion. I'd gone out celebrating afterward with some friends. I was intending to sleep all morning. But then, the phone rang.

(*Sound of a telephone. Bernstein pantomimes picking up a phone.*)

Bernstein: Hello? Yes? What time is it? Yes it is. Who? Who? What! Oh, dear God! I'll be there right away!

Walter: Sick as I was, I told them to tell Lenny to come by my room. The least I could do was go through the scores with him.

Bernstein: Maestro, Maestro! Are you all right? You look terrible!

Walter: (*Speaking in a weak voice.*) I've been better. I certainly can't stand on the podium today and conduct.

Bernstein: Are you sure?

Walter: I'm positive! Besides, you're ready to go on.

Bernstein: No, I'm not. What about Rodzinski? Shouldn't we call him?

Walter: It's only two hours until the concert. He could never make it back in time. Besides . . . he knows.

Rodzinski: (*Miming phone.*) This is what? Who? Bruno Walter is ill? Impossible! The conductor of a major philharmonic orchestra never becomes ill! The doctor said? You're sure? I can't make it there! You will have to . . . call Bernstein. He'll have to go on.

Bernstein: And he had confidence in me? To go on?

Walter: We all do, Lenny. You must. This is your fate. Today shall be your public debut as a conductor!

Bernstein: I . . . I will do my best, Maestro. Please feel better.

(Walter and Rodzinski exit.)

Bernstein: I didn't know if I should laugh or cry . . . or pray. I went to Carnegie Hall. I put on a jacket. The musicians were on stage warming up. The audience came. The curtain opened. I took a deep breath and . . .

(Bernstein turns away from the audience, waves his arms as if conducting. Music begins Strauss's "Don Quixote." Bernstein "conducts" for several minutes. Music fades out. The ensemble of actors backstage claps loudly, shouts, "Bravo!" Bernstein turns toward to the audience and bows.)

Bernstein: Thank you! Thank you!

(Suddenly, Bernstein is swamped by fans who want autographs and by reporters who want to talk with him. His Mother and Father stand off to the side.)

Fan 1: How fabulous! That was the most energetic conducting I've ever seen!

Fan 2: The Philharmonic hasn't seen anything like this in years!

Reporter 1: Mr. Bernstein, Mr. Bernstein, I'm from the *New York Post*. I'd like to do a feature on you for the music page. It'll say, "Young Maestro Steals the Show!"

Reporter Two: I'm from *The New York Times*. Forget the music page — let's talk about the front page!

Bernstein: Here, and here, and here are your autographs. And you, can I call you tomorrow? Please everyone. It has been a rather long and exhausting day!

(Everyone but Bernstein's parents exit. They embrace him.)

Mother: Leonard, my Leonard! What joy you've brought us!

Father: Who knew my son would turn out to be Leonard Bernstein!

Mother: All those years, banging away on Aunt Rose's piano paid off. At least I know my sleepless nights contributed to something great!

Bernstein: Mama, Papa, I'm so happy you were here today to see me realize my dream.

Father: My son, I couldn't be prouder of you in any way. You have become what you were born to do. You create music that captures the spirit. It is truly a gift from God.

Bernstein: So you wouldn't be happier if I were a Rabbi?

Father: Anyone can become a Rabbi. There's only one Leonard Bernstein in the world.

Mother: Come, you must be hungry. Let's go out and get something to eat! New York has so many nice restaurants.

(Mother and Father exit. Bernstein stays, center stage.)

Bernstein: That day, Leonard Bernstein the conductor was born. I was critically praised in the newspapers. I was the talk of the town. People who had never been to a

concert hall before started coming to the Philharmonic.
They wanted to see this young American conductor for
themselves.

(*Enter Rodzinski.*)

Rodzinski: I never knew what all the fuss was about!
Yes, Bernstein was young, talented, but the way people
were talking! They were swelling his head — making him
think he was God!

(*He exits.*)

Bernstein: Rodzinski never accepted the attention I
received. No matter. I soon took a job as Music Director
for the New York Symphony. I was also working hard as a
composer. And the biggest thrill of my life — in 1947, I
was guest conductor for a Jewish Symphony in Palestine
. . . soon to be Israel.

(*Felicia enters.*)

Felicia: In 1951, Lenny married me, Felicia Montealegre
Cohn, an actress from South America. When Lenny and I
first met, I knew we would be together. I loved his
brilliance. I did not think of him as a world famous
conductor and composer. I only thought of him as my
love, my husband.

(*Jamie, Alexander, and Nina enter.*)

Jamie: Our Father? We knew Daddy was famous. When
I was a little girl, he composed the music for *West Side
Story*. It became a huge Broadway hit! That means even
people who didn't follow the New York symphony scene
soon heard of Leonard Bernstein! He became known all
over America!

(Music plays "America" from West Side Story. *The Bernstein family dances together on stage, laughing and playing around.)*

Nina: What mattered most is Daddy liked to play with us, read with us, swim with us, listen to us. Only when I was older did I find out what an unusual Dad I had.

(The family exits, except for Alexander.)

Alexander: Dad, do we have to study?

Bernstein: Alexander, next year you will become a Bar Mitzvah. That means you will be seen as an adult in the eyes of the Jewish community. As a father, I have a responsibility to pass on our rich and wonderful heritage. Now, open up your Chumash.

Alexander: But why do I need to know this stuff? It's not like I'm going to become a Rabbi or something.

Bernstein: You never know. Your great-grandfather was a very respected Hasidic Rabbi. Maybe it's in your genes . . . your destiny.

Alexander: You studied for your Bar Mitzvah, but you don't need to know that stuff now. You don't read from the Torah. You don't lead services.

Bernstein: Maybe not. And when I was your age, I resented having to study with my father, too. I didn't know what the Torah, the Talmud had to do with my life. Only as I grew older did I understand how valuable it was to have studied Jewish texts, to learn to understand the Jewish mind. I am not a Rabbi, Alexander, but I am a Jewish composer. You hear the Jewish tradition in my music. It is an integral part of my soul. Music is full of stories, of language, of philosophy. This heritage is a gift for you, Alexander, just as it was for me.

Alexander: So when we're done, can we go out for a bike ride?

Bernstein: It's a deal!

(Music begins to play Bernstein's Kaddish. *Bernstein stands and turns away from the audience. Alexander faces the audience and speaks.)*

Alexander: My Father, Leonard Bernstein, died in 1990. During his life, he achieved worldwide recognition as a composer, conductor, pianist, author, and teacher. One of his greatest joys was conducting the Israel Philharmonic in the newly formed Jewish State. All around the world today, his works for theater and orchestra are played constantly. The music of Leonard Bernstein, my father, a great Jewish American composer, lives on.

(Alexander exits. Bernstein turns toward the audience and bows.)

Leonard Bernstein is regarded as one of America's most respected conductors, composers, and pianists. He was Music Director of the New York Symphony Orchestra from 1945 to 1947, and was appointed Music Director of the New York Philharmonic in 1958. His "Young People's Concerts," which extended over 14 seasons, introduced many children to classical music. Bernstein's versatile musical talents were displayed in his wide range of compositions. He wrote both popular and serious music, including many works with Jewish themes – Symphony No. 1, Jeremiah; *Symphony*

No. 3, Kaddish, *(which was premiered by the Israel Philharmonic Orchestra and dedicated to the memory of John F. Kennedy); and* The Chichester Psalms. *His contributions to the Broadway musical stage include* On the Town, Wonderful Town, Candide, *and the landmark musical* West Side Story. *He was sought after as a guest conductor by orchestras all over the world. He had a strong influence on American musical taste, and he made over 400 recordings. Leonard Bernstein died of a heart attack in 1990; he was 72 years old.*

Emma Goldman: The Life of a Jewish Anarchist

Characters*

Emma Goldman
Helena Goldman
Mother
Father
Passengers
Immigration Official
Secretary
Leopold Garson
Workers
Prosecutor
Lawyer
Judge
Rosie
Susannah
Agnes
Doctor
Max
Harry
Alice
J. Edgar Hoover

*One actor can play more than one character if necessary.

Costumes

This play takes place in the late nineteenth and early twentieth centuries. Some students could research and construct simple costumes representing these times. The play could also be produced with all the actors wearing simple black dresses and/or shirts and pants.

Setting

The play can be produced using few set pieces — several chairs, tables, etc. The dialogue should move the play from scene to scene and thus capture the imagination of the audience.

Scene 1. St. Petersburg, Russia, 1885.

(Helena Goldman is onstage alone. She paces back and forth and calls for her younger sister.)

Helena: Emma! Emma! Where are you? We should have been home by now! Mama will have a fit! Emmmmaaaa!

(Emma Goldman enters.)

Emma: Helena, why are you screaming? I'm here.

Helena: I couldn't find you! And we're late! We told Mama we'd finish the shopping and be home to help in the store. Look, it's way past when we said we'd meet!

Emma: Don't worry. I'll take the blame . . . as usual. Mama won't get angry with you.

Helena: I don't want you to get in trouble . . . again.

Emma: What can Papa do, give me another beating? So what? He can hurt my body, but he can't touch my soul.

Helena: Emma, you are so headstrong! How did you become so brave?

Emma: I'm not so brave, Helena. I just have to fight for what I believe in. If I didn't speak my mind, I'd die!

Helena: You might just die some day from speaking your mind! If Papa's temper gets too . . .

Emma: I have no fear of Papa at all! Helena, you know the story from the Apocrypha about Judith? Judith is the avenger. She cuts off her enemy's head and runs with it through the streets!

Helena: I remember us reading it together.

Emma: With so many enemies today, I need to be a Judith, too. There are anti-Semites here in Russia including the entire government, which won't let a Jew earn a decent living or attend the university. The Tsar is the worst anti-Semite of all. Then we have enemies who hold us back because we're women! There are those who think all women are stupid, and so we are deprived of a good education! We suffer, Helena, just because we are Jews and just because we are women. You and I can understand suffering — the suffering of the poor who have no way to earn a living. I was late tonight because I was at a meeting.

Helena: What kind of meeting?

Emma: A meeting of radicals — people who want to fight against the status quo, against authority. People who believe that we can bridge the gulf between corruption and justice, that we can make a difference.

Helena: Emma, you know what happens to people who go to those meetings. They are taken away to places . . . like Siberia!

Emma: I will have to risk that.

Helena: I know a better way, Emma. I want to go to America and live with our sister Lena. We've been writing. Look, I have her letters right here. She says I could come and stay with her. There's plenty of work there, and young girls like us can earn our own living. I want freedom, too. Emma. Only I couldn't leave Russia without you. I would be sick from worrying.

Emma: Lena would never have me stay with her. She's as bad as Mother. She hates me.

Helena: Look here, Emma. Read! See . . . she says, "Emma can come, too."

Emma: I don't believe it.

Helena: We would be together in the land of freedom. You could go to your meetings there and no one would ever bother you.

Emma: There are many radical circles in America. There are workers who join together to fight for better conditions.

Helena: You will be a leader there, Emma. I know you! I can see it!

Emma: There are no serious occupations for me here in Russia, Helena. My hope for a higher education has been crushed. Since I was a little girl, I dreamed of becoming a doctor, of healing people. When I passed the entrance exam to University, I was shocked! Rarely does a Jewish girl pass, but then that horrible teacher refused to write the necessary recommendation letter! On his authority I was denied entrance to the University. Now I know, not only people get sick, but nations are sick, too. Russia is sick with corruption. American is a young land, with promise. Oh, Helena, I want to go!

(They embrace.)

Helena: When we get home, let me do the talking. Please. I can convince Papa.

Emma: Even if Moses came down from Mt. Sinai and landed in our living room, he couldn't change Papa's mind!

Helena: We'll try, Emma. We'll try.

Scene 2. Later that evening, in the Goldman's home.

Helena *(Entering.)*: SSShhh. Emma, Mama's in the store and no one else is around. Let's sneak into the kitchen and . . .

Emma: Uh-oh.

Father: *(Entering from the other side of the stage.)* No one's around but your Father! Where have you girls been? It's not respectable for two young girls to gallivant around at this time of night.

Helena: Papa, we're not so young anymore.

Father: Don't remind me! *(Grabs Emma by the ear.)* And let me guess — it was this one who was out causing trouble!

Emma: Oww! Let me go!

Helena: Wait, Papa, I was responsible! I ran into . . . an acquaintance I haven't seen in quite some time and . . .

Father: Don't lie, Helena! You've become as bad as your rotten sister.

Emma: *(Emma pushes her father away.)* Don't put your hands on me! I am leaving this house as soon as I can!

Helena: Emma, let me explain what . . .

Father: Leaving, are you? Well, I see we agree on something at last. You will be leaving soon. There's only one thing to do with an impudent young thing like you: marry her off. That's right. Shut your jaws, girls. I've made arrangements for Emma to be wed.

Emma: But I'm only 15!

Father: An old maid.

Emma: But I don't want to get married! I want to study. I want to read! I've just started reading Turgenev!

Father: Turgenev, indeed. Here's what studying will get you!

(He takes Emma's book from her and throws it into the fireplace.)

Helena: Papa! Into the fire? How could you? How cruel!

Father: Our little Emma needs to learn . . . that a Jewish daughter doesn't need to know more than how to prepare gefilte fish, to cut noodles fine, and to give her man plenty of children.

(Mother enters.)

Mother: The cats have finally come home. Is that what all this fussing is about?

Helena: Papa threw Emma's book in the fire . . . and he's arranged a marriage for her! To someone she doesn't know or love!

Mother: Love? What's that got to do with marriage? You girls make your heads foolish with your new books. Well, with Emma gone, it will be one less mouth to feed.

Emma: Helena and I both work — we bring in most of the money around here! We knit shawls all day until our fingers are numb. You know that, Mother.

Helena: I've had word from Lena. She invited Emma and me to America, to come stay with her as long as we'd like. We want to go. We want to go to the land of the free.

Mother: Lena invited Emma? You're joking.

Helena: I said I wouldn't leave without Emma. And I won't.

Father: Then you'll both stay right here in St. Petersburg. Emma is getting married.

Emma: No, Papa! I am going with Helena to America!

Father: You are staying here!

Emma: You can't stop me. I'll sneak away.

Father: I'll take you right now to the Rabbi. You can get married tonight.

Emma: And if you do that . . . I will jump into the river and drown in my wedding dress. In the morning, everyone will say Abraham Goldman's daughter committed suicide. They'll whisper it in hushed tones. There will be shame in people's eyes when they pass you in the street. Customers will walk by this sad little store. I will do it, Papa. I will jump in the river if you don't let me go to America. You know I will.

(There is silence in the room.)

Father: Don't give them any money, Mother. They are grown-up girls. They can get to America with their own money.

(Lights down.)

Scene 3. On the boat. Emma and Helena have almost reached America.

Helena: Emma, wake up! Look in the distance! I can see the shore!

Emma: Let me sleep, Helena. I couldn't sleep at all last night. The ship was rocking back and forth.

Helena: You'll have time to sleep later — in America! Emma, we've almost made it. We've survived this boat ride, the horrid food, and the seasickness.

Emma: We haven't survived it yet!

Helena: Look, Emma. In the distance I see a great statue rising from the water.

Emma: That's her! Lady Liberty! I just read an article about her. She is a gift from France. She is set there in the harbor to welcome new arrivals to America — like us, Helena.

Passenger 1: Excuse me. Do you know when we finally land in America?

Helena: It should be any moment now.

Passenger 1: My children have been sick, this whole boat ride. They need medicine.

Emma: Here, I have an orange. Let them suck on it. That will make them feel better.

Passenger 1: Thank you, miss.

Emma: In America, they can go to a doctor. They'll be well in no time.

Passenger 2: Get your bags! Get your bags! I see people lining up on the deck! We'll be arriving in America soon!

Passenger 3: I can't wait to see it! I've dreamed of it for so long! Streets paved with gold!

Passenger 2: In America, everyone is rich!

Passenger 1: And healthy!

Passenger 3: And strong!

Helena: Emma, it's true — we're here at last!

Emma: We are free, Helena. We are safe in liberty's arms now.

(An immigration official enters.)

Official: You have just landed in Castle Garden. Get in a straight line, single file! Get your papers out! No talking1 No moving! Stay in line!

Passenger 2: What is he saying? I don't know English!

Official: (*Grabs him and pushes him.*) End of the line for you, buddy! I said Quiet! Orders are orders!

Passenger 1: Officer, my children are sick as you can see. Can't we go ahead?

Official: Sick kids? Here's a paper for you, lady. We don't want sickness brought in here. You can go right back to where you came from.

Passenger 1: But I don't have any money! My brother is waiting to meet us.

Official: Not my problem.

Emma: Helena, I can't believe this — did you hear what he said?

Helena: Shhh, Emma. He said we must be quiet.

Emma: But this is just like Russia! What kind of freedom is this?

Helena: Be patient, Emma. Please. Things are not always what they seem.

Official: Step forward! Straight line! Papers out! You dirty miserable animals. You filth!

Helena: Quiet, Emma. Quiet now. Please . . . just for me.

(Emma and Helena are at the front of the line. The Official waves them ahead. They exit.)

Scene 4. Six months later, the office of Leopold Garson in Rochester, New York.

Secretary: Mr. Garson, this is Emma Goldman, the worker who wished to speak with you. She's been working in your factory for four months.

Garson: Yes. Bring her in.

Emma: Mr. Garson.

Garson: Miss Goldman.

Emma: What beautiful red roses you have on your desk — American Beauty roses. I saw such roses in the window of a flower shop the other day. I went in to buy some, but found I didn't have enough money to buy even one!

Garson: What is it you want, Miss Goldman?

Emma: I've been working here for four months, Mr. Garson – ever since I arrived with my younger sister from St. Petersburg. In Russia I worked in a factory, too. I was so excited to come to Rochester, New York, to work for you, a Jewish man, Mr. Leopold Garson. There weren't any Jewish factory owners in Russia.

Garson: I am a German Jew. I don't know how you do business in Russia.

Emma: But conditions are worse here. In St. Petersburg we could sing and talk to pass the time while we work.

Here we must be silent. I need permission to go to the restroom! It's impossible to live like this.

Garson: I run my factory as efficiently as possible. This is a factory, not a dance hall.

Emma: Which brings me to my point, Mr. Garson. I can't live on the wages you pay! I have no money left over to buy a book or to see a movie or to go dancing. I pay room and board to my older sister and need carfare for work. There's nothing left after that.

Garson: You have expensive tastes, Miss Goldman. If you don't like working here, I suggest you find employment somewhere else. My other workers never complain.

Emma: They're afraid to — they need their wages! But a person should have more for working so hard — money for clothes and books and . . . and roses! You grow richer by the day while those of us in the factory have less and less.

Garson: The door is behind you, Miss Goldman. I'm a very busy man, so you'll kindly excuse me. Good day.

Emma: I quit, Mr. Garson. You just wait. There'll be more like me.

(Emma exits dramatically. Garson sighs and goes back to his papers. Lights down.)

Scene 5. Four years later.

(Emma is alone onstage writing a letter to Helena.)

Emma: My dear Helena. It is hard to believe four years have passed since I left Rochester. After my quick marriage ended in divorce, the Jews of Rochester made me feel as though I were a pariah. I do not miss those narrow-minded thinkers; all I miss of Rochester is you. (*Pause.*) I am gaining quite a reputation here in New York City and in the national press as well. I am asked to speak often, and many come to hear my message.

Helena, I believe so strongly in anarchy. We as individuals must rise up and free ourselves from the constraints of oppressive government. We thought America would be the land of opportunity, but it is a land of oppression, just like Russia. Millions of people slave away in factories, coal mines, steel mills, sweatshops for pennies a day, while the few get rich. I dream of individuals finding the spirit of revolution . . . rising up and creating a new culture . . . rooted in freedom, without compulsion, without authority. I am giving my life to this dream, Helena. I hope you understand.

Scene 6. Union Square, New York City, 1893.

(Emma stands on a "soapbox" and "preaches" to a large crowd, which responds with cheers.)

Emma: My friends, America is in an economic depression. Unemployment is at an all-time high with four million people out of work. They have no way of providing for their families. Is this any surprise? I think not! Our society is ordered to oppress the worker; our government does not care if workers starve! The state legislature of New York has not acted to help our homeless and hungry. My friends, we cannot trust politicians to help us. We must stand up and demand what is ours. The starving must demand bread! If they won't give you bread, you must steal bread! It is your basic human rights we are fighting for today!

(The crowd cheers loudly, waves their arms. They exit the stage shouting, "Bread! Bread! Bread!")

Scene 7. Emma is in court, arrested for inciting a riot.

Judge: The prosecutor may call another witness to the stand.

Prosecutor: Your Honor, I would like to call the defendant, Emma Goldman, to the stand.

(Emma goes to the stand.)

Prosecutor: I have a few questions for you, Miss Goldman.

Emma: I am prepared to tell the truth.

Prosecutor: Do you believe in a Supreme Being, Miss Goldman?

Emma: What does this have to do with my arrest? I am being charged with three counts of inciting a riot. This trial is not about my personal beliefs!

Judge: Answer the question, Miss Goldman.

Prosecutor: Do you believe in a Supreme Being, Miss Goldman?

Emma: No, sir, I do not.

Prosecutor: Is there any government on earth whose laws you approve of?

Emma: No sir, all governments are basically against the people.

Prosecutor: Why don't you leave this country if you don't like its laws?

Emma: Where shall I go? Everywhere on earth the laws are against the poor, and they tell me I cannot go to heaven . . . nor do I want to go there.

Prosecutor: No further questions.

Judge: You may take your seat, Miss Goldman. The jury will discuss the evidence and we will reconvene shortly.

Emma: (*To her lawyer.*) This isn't a fair trial! I'm being judged on my beliefs, not my actions.

Lawyer: Emma, what did you expect? I am beginning to agree with you. The government is corrupt. It does not protect the people!

Judge: Order in the court! The jury has made their decision.

Jury: We declare that Emma Goldman, an atheist and anarchist, is guilty of inciting the people to riot in Union Square!

Judge: I hereby declare that Emma Goldman must serve one year in Blackwell Prison for this crime against society. Miss Goldman, it is clear that you are a woman of above average intelligence, but those who do not believe in the law cannot be trusted. I hope your prison term will teach you a valuable lesson. Observance of the law is an absolute necessity.

(Lights down.)

Scene 8. Blackwell Prison, the infirmary.

(Emma is serving as prison nurse. Several women are there for treatment.)

Emma: Here's your medication, Rosie. Wash it down with lots of water . . . that's right. In no time, you'll be free of fever.

Rosie: Thanks, Miss Emma. You always make me feel better.

Emma: Just rest now. Okay, Susannah, let's see that wound. Ah, it's getting better. I'm going to change the bandage now. I don't want you to get an infection.

Susannah: I thought I'd surely die from this knife wound, Miss Emma. My husband, he's come at me before, but never like this time. I hit him with a lamp just to keep him off me. I never thought I'd knock him out.

Emma: You clearly hurt him in self-defense. It's insane that the government has locked you up! What were you supposed to do — let him kill you?

Susannah: I've been listening to you, Miss Emma. I think you're onto something. The government doesn't make it easy on a woman.

Emma: Before I was sent to prison, I was concerned with the idea of injustice. But in the last year, I have seen injustice, I have lived with it, and I know it intimately. This government is cruel and oppressive to women. Look at you, for example — a woman beaten by her husband who has nowhere to go.

Susannah: When you get out, you keep preaching. People gotta listen to you.

Emma: Rest now. That's good. Who's next?

Agnes: Can you help me, ma'am?

Emma: What is it? What's wrong?

Agnes: I have pains. I get pains all the time. Since my last baby, they don't go away. The doctor told me not to have more children, but I couldn't help it.

Emma: How many children do you have?

Agnes: Eight. With each one, the pains got worse. Now I have 'em all the time.

Emma: Lie back, dear. The doctor should be here soon.

(The Prison Doctor enters.)

Emma: I have a woman here who needs your help, Doctor. She has severe pains.

Doctor: I'll be right with her, but first a question for you.

Emma: Yes?

Doctor: Emma, I just learned that your sentence is over next week.

Emma: One whole year has finally passed!

Doctor: Emma, you're one of the finest nurses I've ever worked with. I don't want to lose you. When you leave here, I want you to continue to work as my nurse . . . in my private practice. Will you?

Emma: Of course I will! This work is so satisfying. But will your patients mind being cared for by Red Emma Goldman?

Doctor: They should be honored to be treated by you.

Emma: Good enough. I suppose I can be both an anarchist and a nurse.

Doctor: Only you, Emma. Now, back to our patients.

(Emma leads the Doctor to Agnes. Lights down.)

Scene 9. 12 years later, 1906.

(Helena is alone on stage, writing a letter to Emma.)

Helena: My dearest Emma. It is hard to believe we've been in America over 20 years now. I still remember — as if it was yesterday — our long ride on the boat. I remember the nights, curled up beside you in our little bunk. With you next to me, I knew I was safe. My brave Emma. America has not been the dream we thought it would be. I read about you in the newspaper today. The press vilifies you, Emma. They draw horrible caricatures of you. They call you a national enemy! I want to shout to the world — "Stop! Emma is my little sister. Emma is kind and giving. Emma is a nurse who goes to the homes of the wretched poor whenever they call for her!" But your speeches frighten people. You talk about birth control and how women should have choice in how many children they will have. I agree. Poor families can't feed lots of children. You say that marriage makes women lifelong dependents. That is true, as well. We were raised in an unhappy marriage. Everyone was miserable. I admire your ideas, Emma. But I am scared for you. I am scared of the way those journalists write about you. I wish the world could know my Emma. Yours forever, Helena.

Scene 10. Emma's office.

(Emma is having a meeting with several anarchist friends.)

Emma: Thank you for meeting here this morning. I have good news.

Max: Emma, I haven't seen you this excited in years.

Emma: There's a good reason to be excited! I know how to get our message out to America.

Harry: We've been doing that! We make speeches wherever we can. People flock to meet the real Red Emma Goldman!

Emma: I want to reach more people on a larger scale. I want to connect radical thinkers worldwide. I want a vehicle through which anarchist writers can publish their work.

Alice: Good luck! The only way we can publish our work is to print our own pamphlets.

Emma: Exactly! But we don't need to limit ourselves to pamphlets. I see a magazine, a journal, that will showcase our ideology . . .

Max: Emma, Emma! Have you any idea what such an endeavor would cost?

Harry: Stop dreaming. We could never afford such a thing.

Emma: Now we can! A very successful actor friend of mine, who supports our cause, is ready to make a sizeable donation. We can do it! Imagine, a radical journal for all America! For the entire world!

Alice: Emma, you are something else — unstoppable! What will we call the journal?

Emma: I've thought about calling it "Mother Earth." That is our dream, after all — to find a way to live in harmony with the earth, to make the earth a livable place for all people.

Max: This calls for a toast! To Mother Earth!

Everyone: To Mother Earth!

(Lights down.)

Scene 11. Rochester, 1917.

(Emma and Helena meet in Rochester.)

Helena: Where is she? Where could she be? I'm getting worried. Emma!

Emma: (*Entering.*) Helena! Here I am! Oh, it's so good to see you!

Helena: Here it is, 1917. You are 48 years old. And I still worry about you as if you were 16, and out getting into trouble somewhere.

Emma: Trouble has always followed me, Helena. We know that by now.

Helena: What time does your speech start? Can you come have dinner with me first?

Emma: Let's meet afterward. I need to change my speech somewhat.

Helena: But, Emma, why? Birth control and women's rights. You've been crusading all over the country to get information about these issues to the people. You've gone to prison for speaking about these subjects — countless times! Don't give up on them now!

Emma: I'll touch upon them, Helena. I'm not giving up those causes. It's just that I need to speak about more pressing issues.

Helena: Emma, no, please, not what I'm thinking!

Emma: President Wilson was elected on a platform to keep America out of this war. Militarism is killing thousands of innocent Prussians and Germans. If America enters the war, thousands of innocent Americans will die . . . and for what? Nationalistic pride?

Helena: Emma, war is serious business. Too serious even for you. Tonight you must lecture on birth control. Please stay away from these other matters.

Emma: I've always spoken my conscience, Helena. And I've urged others to do the same. We are told we have free speech in America, yet I've been jailed repeatedly for speaking my mind. If they send me to jail again, so be it.

Helena: I don't want you to go to jail. I don't want you to suffer.

Emma: Everyone lives in a jail, Helena . . . everyone who can't speak their mind. I cannot and do not condone the draft of innocent American men into the military!

Helena: Emma, I don't know how to tell you this. I don't know how to say it . . .

Emma: What, Helena? What is it?

Helena: I have a bad feeling. I don't know why. Something is troubling my soul. It's about you. You're not safe. Something bad will happen.

(Emma embraces Helena.)

Emma: Don't worry about me, Helena. Whatever happens to me is not important. I fight for causes greater than my own life. I haven't believed in God for years, but I do believe in the Jewish teaching — "Justice, justice shall you pursue."

Helena: You are my Judith! You will avenge the enemy for your people.

Emma: Through it all, I love you, Helena. I can't imagine doing anything without your support.

(They embrace again.)

Helena: I'll see you after your speech. Good luck, Emma.

(Lights down.)

Scene 12. A courtroom, 1919.

(Emma is on trial for advocating revolution.)

J. Edgar Hoover: Miss Goldman. You have just been released from two years in prison, for inciting American citizens to resist the draft. The war is now over and America's role in the war was vital. In hindsight, do you believe you were wrong?

Emma: No, Mr. Hoover. I do not believe in military allegiance to any country or its government that does not care for the welfare of its citizens.

Hoover: And you believe the American government has no such regard for its citizens?

Emma: In all my years in America, I have spoken out for the poor and the oppressed. American citizens labor away for meager wages, while a select few get richer and richer. American women have more children than their bodies or their pocketbooks can handle, because the government won't allow information about birth control to be distributed. Free speech, which should be protected in your constitution, is a federal offense, for which I've been jailed. While I was in prison this last time, I had the opportunity to meet with poor colored women. They have been oppressed more than anyone else because of racism in America. I advocate abolishing this government and forming a new culture in which all human beings have the opportunity to earn a decent wage and be free.

Hoover: Is it true that you belong to organizations that advocate revolution?

Emma: The revolution that I described above, yes.

Hoover: And is it also true that you are not a citizen of the United States?

Emma: I am a citizen of the world. I have not officially applied for citizenship to this country. I have lived here since I was 16 years old.

Judge: As you know, Miss Goldman, a new law has been passed, which gives us the right to deport any illegal immigrant who belongs to organizations that support revolution and sabotage. Prison has not reformed you. There is nothing to be done now, but send you away.

Emma: Deportation? But my home is here . . . my friends . . . my family . . . my magazine, "Mother Earth."

Judge: Perhaps you should have thought of this before now, Miss Goldman. You and your anarchist friends will be deported immediately!

Hoover: Justice is served.

Emma: Because in America, justice is not blind.

(Lights down.)

Scene 13. At the dock.

(Emma is about to board the ship that will take her away to Russia. Helena comes to say good-bye.)

Emma: Where is she? Where could she be? The ship will be leaving soon.

Helena: (*Entering.*) Emma! Here I am! They wouldn't tell me where you were.

Emma: That's the government — to the last moment, trying to break my spirit.

Helena: Look what I've brought you. Blankets so you won't be cold. Crackers and tins of fish . . . and I baked you a bread. Smell, it's still hot.

Emma: You don't forget a thing!

Helena: Emma. How strange this is! Coming to Ellis Island to say good-bye.

Emma: Lady Liberty stands here, but her torch has gone out.

Helena: She is not the true Lady Liberty. My Emma is!

Emma: I will write you, Helena. Hopefully, my letters will be delivered.

Helena: Where will you be writing from? Where are they taking you?

Emma: The rumor is Russia. But wherever I end up, I'll be fine. Don't you worry. I'm with my friends.

Helena: I wish I could go with you.

Emma: Your family is here. Don't think of it. Don't worry. This isn't good-bye. I'll be back, Helena. I hate the government, but I love America. The people, their spirit, all the wonderful Americans I have come to know and love — this I will miss.

Helena: I know you'll find a way to return.

Emma: The Jewish people have always lived in exile and we have survived. I'm in good company, Helena. Don't you worry about me.

Helena: Good-bye, Emma. Be safe. Good-bye.

(They embrace.)

Immigration Official: All aboard! You there — get your bags and get on that ship!

Helena: You are talking to my sister, the world famous Emma Goldman! Mind your manners! Can't you behave like a human being?

Official: I — I'm sorry, Ma'am.

(Emma turns to board the ship. She stops and looks back. She thumbs her nose as she speaks.)

Emma: Good-bye, America! Good-bye!

(She takes her bags and exits. Lights down.)

*In 1919, dynamic activist/anarchist **Emma Goldman** was deported to Russia, along with 247 other "subversive aliens." She soon became disillusioned with the revolution there and left two years later. She spent the remaining years of her life traveling and living in a number of countries including Sweden, Germany, England, Spain, and Canada. She continued to agitate, sometimes ending up in prison and always giving her life and energies to her ideals. Besides numerous pamphlets, her writings include* Anarchism and Other

Essays, My Disillusionment with Russia, *and her autobiography,* Living My Life. *Ms. Goldman is remembered for her work in favor of birth control, among many other causes. She joined the anti-fascist cause in Spain during the civil war there. She died in Canada in 1940, and is buried in Chicago.*

Abraham Joshua Heschel: A Modern Prophet

Characters

Narrator*
Rabbi Heschel
Dr. Martin Luther King, Jr.
Civil Rights Activist 1
Civil Rights Activist 2
Civil Rights Activist 3
Civil Rights Activist 4
Mother
Young Heschel
Melamed
Cheder boys
Moishe
Wife

*The Narrator takes on many guises within this play. The Civil Rights Activists act as a chorus in the classical sense, guiding the play along and commenting on its action. The Narrator often instigates response from them.

Costumes

Rabbi Heschel should wear the big white beard for which he was known. He should dress in a suit and tie, and his head should be covered with a *yarmulke*. Dr. King should also wear a suit and tie. Research clothes from the sixties for the other characters.

Setting

Use a bare stage, because this play has frequent changes of location. This will allow the audience to imagine movement from place to place. Painted backdrops that could be easily put up and removed would help to set the locale for each scene.

(A chorus of Civil Rights Activists walks onto the stage. They stand together and sing, 'We Shall Overcome.')

Chorus: We shall overcome, we shall overcome.
We shall overcome some day.
Oh deep in my heart, I do believe
That we shall overcome some day.

Activist 1: The year is 1965. Over 100 years since the Civil War between the North and the South was fought. Today, the United States of America are anything but united.

Activist 2: We are fighting for basic civil rights — the right to buy decent houses.

Activist 3: Send our children to decent schools.

Activist Four: Vote. We are fighting for the right to vote!

(Narrator enters, stares at them as an onlooker.)

Narrator: Schools, homes, the right to vote? Come on, your kids have schools, you can live anywhere you want. It's a free country. White or Black. Anyone can vote!

Activist 1: That's not true! In many places in America, real estate agents will not sell homes to Black people.

Activist 2: There are no "separate but equal facilities." The public schools which many Black children attend are inadequate — they lack books, they lack heat. Some of them lack running water.

Activist 3: Not to mention that all over the South, there are separate public drinking fountains and toilets. Have you ever stepped inside restrooms marked "Colored"? No one bothers to clean them.

Activist 4: Try drinking from a "Colored" fountain. Hardly a trickle of dirty water comes out.

Narrator: So why are you out in the streets bothering us about all this? What can we do to change this situation? Tell your representatives . . . tell the officials.

Activist 3: We're trying. We're trying to get them to listen to us. That's why we're out here!

Activist 4: Many Black people can't elect the officials they want 'cause they don't have the right to vote! Counties down here pass "Jim Crow" laws — laws they make up that keep us from voting for one reason or another. Then there's intimidation. You ever tried to vote at a place where the Klan was standing outside, in their hoods?

Narrator: So you're just . . . gonna keep singing and marching till you change all that?

Activists: (*Together.*) YES!

(*They sing "We Shall Overcome" again, until the Narrator, frustrated, leaves.*)

Activist 1: Ten years ago, in 1955, in Montgomery, Alabama, a Black woman named Rosa Parks was riding the bus home from work.

Activist 2: The bus driver asked her to stand up and give her seat to a white person.

Activist 3: But that day, Rosa Parks was tired. Tired of being treated like a second-class citizen, tired of being denied basic rights. On that day, when the bus driver asked her to get up and move, Rosa Parks said, "No!"

Activist 4: There happened to be, in Montgomery, Alabama, a young minister named Dr. Martin Luther King, Jr.

Activist 1: When he heard that Rosa Parks had been arrested and put in jail for refusing to give up her seat, he organized protests. He organized the Black community to boycott the buses until the rules were changed.

(Dr. King enters. Narrator follows behind him.).

King: No matter what happens, we must remember the words of the Bible, "Love your enemies."

Narrator: But the police have billy clubs! They have dogs ready to attack us! How can we love them, Reverend King. How can we love them when they're trying to hurt us?

King: We must be strong, we must be compassionate. No matter how they try to hurt us, we must believe, "Love your enemies."

(Dr. King stands center stage.)

Activist 2: All over the South, Dr. King started leading similar boycotts and protests. He galvanized people who had been oppressed.

Activist 3: We began to speak out! We began to demand our rights!

Activist 4: Dr. King, through it all, remained a man of deep religious conviction.

Activist 1: I wish I could say the same for most "religious" people.

Activist 2: Yes, where were they? Where were they when we were putting our lives on the line? Where were the other preachers, ministers, priests, and Rabbis?

Activist 3: Doesn't their Bible say, "Love your neighbor as yourself"?

Activist 4: Where were they during our marches, during the sit-ins? They were sitting in their churches and synagogues, nice and safe.

King: No! No! They joined us, they helped us, they supported us . . . after one man spoke.

Narrator: The year is 1963. The place is the National Conference on Religion and Race. A Rabbi named Dr. Abraham Joshua Heschel was asked to give the keynote address.

(Dr. Heschel enters and stands center stage, alongside Dr. King.)

Heschel: The Negro People in America are like the ancient children of Israel, caught in bondage. We must help them cross the sea — where they can find decent housing, adequate employment, proper education. It is not enough that we pray for change; rather like the great biblical prophets, we must speak out. We must act. Each of us is responsible!

Activist 1: Who is this Rabbi? I've never heard another clergyman besides Dr. King speak this way!

Activist 2: I thought Rabbi Heschel was a scholar, stuck in some ivory tower somewhere!

Activist 3: He is a professor of Jewish ethics and mysticism at the Jewish Theological Seminary.

Activist 4: He has written many influential books in his lifetime — *Man Is Not Alone, God's Search for Man, The Sabbath* . . .

Heschel: I urge each of you as religious leaders to stand up and support Dr. King and the Civil Rights Movement. In our Jewish tradition, we teach that we must be partners with God. The world is not complete; each of us is completing it. It is not up to God to solve our problems. We are created in the Divine Image to act godly, holy . . . toward others. I cannot stand by and watch my fellow human beings treated like animals! I will help the Civil Rights Movement however I am able.

(Rabbi Heschel and Dr. King shake hands. They walk offstage together, talking.)

Activist 1: Rabbi Heschel's speech that night inspired other clergy to take action. Many of those religious leaders joined Dr. King later that year in the March on Washington. Soon, in churches and synagogues across the country, people were speaking out about Civil Rights. It became clear that it was a moral issue, not just a political one.

Narrator: Hold it, hold it right there. Wait just a minute. Who was this Rabbi Heschel? If you ask me, he stirred up a lot of trouble. Don't the Jews have enough to worry about? I mean, it's only been 20 years since the Holocaust. Maybe this Rabbi should have focused on

Jewish problems . . . and let the Black community deal with their own issues.

Activist 2: Dr. Heschel didn't see things in black and white, so to speak. He believed that human beings were responsible for each other.

Activist 3: No matter what religion or race.

Activist 4: All responsible for one another.

Narrator: Humm. He spoke up before the other religious leaders. What was it about him? And how did he get that way?

(The chorus of Activists steps back to the sides of the stage as scenes from Rabbi Heschel's life unfold.)

Activist 1: Let us tell you a bit about the man who spoke up and acted. (*Pause.*) It is pre-war Poland. The year is 1914. Abraham Joshua Heschel is seven years old.

Activist 2: He is part of a large Hasidic family.

(Young Heschel and Mother enter.)

Mother: Abraham Joshua, hurry and eat your breakfast! You'll be late for *cheder* and you have so much to learn there.

Young Heschel: Mama, why do you always call me by two names, Abraham and Joshua?

Mother: Such a question! All the great Rebbes in our family are known by two names. It is a great honor. One day, when you grow up, you will become a great Rebbe, too.

Young Heschel: I don't understand. How do you know I'll be a great Rebbe? Why do I have to become a Rebbe just because Papa is and his Papa was before him?

Mother: It is the Hasidic tradition — we have important family lines that have always produced great leaders for our people. People need leaders, Abraham Joshua. People need moral and spiritual guidance — someone they can turn to. Someone who can help them understand right from wrong.

Young Heschel: How will I learn those things, Mama? What will I teach them?

Mother: You will learn by studying. And not just books. You must study the world around you . . . people and nature itself. God is in everything around us, God calls to us if only we listen. The universe is truly full of God's glory. (*Pause.*) Now grab your books. That's it. Good-bye, Abraham Joshua. Make your Mother proud.

(*Mother exits and other Cheder boys enter, as does the Melamed, the teacher.*)

Melamed: All right, boychicks . . . today we will be learning the *parashah* in which our father Abraham, may his name be blessed, takes his son Isaac to Mount Moriah to be sacrificed. Moishe, you read.

Moishe: . . . And Abraham picked up the knife to slay his son. Then an angel of God called to him from heaven, "Abraham, Abraham!" And he answered, "Here I am." And he said, "Do not raise your hand against the boy or do anything to him. For now I know that you fear God, since you have not withheld your son, your favored one, from Me."

(Young Heschel starts crying softly.)

Melamed: Wait, stop reading Moishe. Abraham Joshua, what's wrong? Why are you crying?

Young Heschel: Just imagine . . . if it had been another moment . . . imagine what would have happened if the angel came too late.

Melamed: Ahh, so that's it. Dry your eyes, Abraham Joshua. I assure you, angels never ever come late.

(They are quiet for a moment.)

Young Heschel: But what about people? What if we don't act fast enough? What if we . . . come late?

(The Melamed stares at his students for a moment. He sighs.)

Melamed: Let's go on. Yaakov, you read.

(They all exit.)

Narrator: A Rebbe? A leader of his people? But Rabbi Heschel — when we saw him — he wasn't a Hasidic Rebbe! He wasn't wearing that black outfit they wear — the big black hat!

Activist 3: He chose not to become the Hasidic Rebbe he was born to be . . . though his Hasidic childhood was always part of him. He became a great spiritual leader, nonetheless, for many people, many Jewish people and people of other faiths and races who read his books.

Activist 4: He was much like a Rebbe in that way.

Narrator: Hasidism seems all right to me. Why did he leave?

(Young Heschel and his Mother enter.)

Young Heschel: Mama, Mama, I'm so glad you're home.

Mother: So where else would I be?

Young Heschel: I have news.

Mother: News? What news?

Young Heschel: I've been accepted. To the University.

(She is silent.)

Young Heschel: I've hesitated telling you and Papa. You may think this move means I'm leaving my faith, but it doesn't. I have learned much in the Hasidic world. I have learned to be in awe of God and creation, that every moment is sacred. I know that, Mama. But these feelings have inspired me to study philosophy and poetry, things I can't learn in the Hasidic world. I will still obey the *mitzvot*, Mama. They are the tools God has given us to make even the most mundane tasks into sacred ones.

Mother: What about your people? What about your responsibility in leading them?

Young Heschel: I know I have responsibilities, Mama. Each of us does. We have responsibilities to help one another, to love our fellow human beings. (*Pause.*) I want to be a leader, Mama. I think I will be someday. Just not now. I need to study first.

Mother: When are you leaving? Where are you going?

Young Heschel: To the University in Berlin. I will start in the fall.

Mother: Your father — how will we tell him?

Young Heschel: Don't worry, Mama. I need to do this. I feel called to go and study. I don't expect Papa to understand.

(They exit.)

Narrator: Berlin? Germany? Wasn't that a dangerous place for a Jew to be? What year is it anyway?

Activist 1: Skip ahead. The year is 1938. The Nazis have risen to power in Germany.

Activist 2: Heschel has earned his doctorate in philosophy from the University of Berlin.

Activist 3: He is just beginning his academic career in Germany . . .

Activist 4: . . . when the Nazis deport all Polish Jews back to Poland.

(Young Heschel enters.)

Young Heschel: This is an outrage! How can the Nazis get away with this? I don't want to leave Berlin. I have a life here, a job, a respected position. Suddenly, I am no longer a Rabbi, no longer a doctor of philosophy. I am simply a number. I am told where to live, what to do. Why is no one speaking out? No one speaking out!

Narrator: But he survives the war, right? I mean we saw him a few minutes ago . . . up there with Dr. King.

Activist 1: He may survive . . .

Activist 2: But the world he knows and cherishes . . .

Activist 3: . . . will not!

Young Heschel: What's this? A letter from Cincinnati, Ohio . . . in America? From Dr. Julius Morgenstern, President of the Hebrew Union College. Why, that's . . . that's the Reform Movement's seminary to train Rabbis in America. What could Dr. Morgenstern want from me? (*Reading.*) "It would be our great honor to invite you, along with a number of eminent Jewish scholars in Europe, to leave the dangerous situation there and come here to our college where you could safely continue your academic work." An offer from America! I have to take it. I know things will get better soon in Europe, but for now, I can't do my work here at all. Dr. Morgenstern, I will gladly accept!

Narrator: So he escapes? To Ohio?

Activist 1: Barely. Two days later, the Nazis invaded Poland. No Jewish person could leave the borders.

Activist 2: Heschel's family, including his mother and sister, were killed by the Nazis.

Activist 3: In America, Heschel could not believe the news reports.

Activist 4: Though he was grateful to Dr. Morgenstern, he did not feel at home at Hebrew Union College. The Reform Movement did not satisfy his spiritual longings. Especially now, with his family, his friends, the life he knew before the Nazis, all gone.

Narrator: So how did he go on? I mean, being a Rabbi? believing in God? Who could believe in God after your family has been killed?

(The older Heschel now takes over the role. He comes on stage with his Wife.)

Wife: I still have hope that we may find your Mother and sister . . . and the rest of the family. People are locating survivors everyday.

Heschel: We can still try, but we have searched everywhere. They are gone from us. We must accept this. May their memories be for a blessing.

Wife: I can't accept it! I don't know how you can — the horrors, the tragedies. We're not the only ones — every Jewish family in Europe was destroyed in some way. So many deaths. Millions. Senseless. (*Pause.*) Abraham, what will you tell people now? How can you comfort them?

Heschel: These questions are not easy to answer. My grief is so deep. Sometimes I fear that I will never pull through it, but I find some inspiration in the words of the ancient prophets.

Wife: Their words apply to this situation — to the Holocaust?

Heschel: They saw horrible destruction, too — the destruction of the Temple, exile, senseless killing of children, starvation. The prophets did not blame God, but people.

Wife: How so?

Heschel: People ask, "Where was God during the Holocaust?" My question is, "Where was Man?" Where was the human outcry? the human outrage? courage? There were righteous gentiles in Europe who risked their lives and saved Jews and others who were pursued by the Nazis. That is true holiness.

Wife: But most people turned a deaf ear. They didn't hear the cries of our people. They simply looked away.

Heschel: This is the "evil of indifference." Though different from the guilt of committing a crime, still, it is evil. We are created in the divine image to take action, to love our fellow human beings. When we look away, as so many people did in Europe . . . we are not acting in accordance with God.

Wife: I understand, I do. It's just not easy . . . to take action.

Heschel: Faith demands action . . . and you're right, it isn't always easy. But it is necessary . . . if we don't want humanity to commit atrocity after atrocity.

Wife: Abraham, when you talk this way about taking action, I start to look around at our own lives. Here we are in New York City. You have a distinguished position teaching at the Jewish Theological Seminary. We have enough money, food, clothes. But so many around us are suffering . . . right here. Don't we need to act on their behalf? Otherwise, aren't we, too, guilty of "the evil of indifference"?

Heschel: Absolutely. It is not enough to be concerned with our own comfort. We have to reach out to those around us in need.

Wife: I will make my life with you one of faith and action. There is so much work to be done . . . to heal the world.

Heschel: We will do all we can together — all that God demands of us.

(They embrace and exit.)

Narrator: I'm starting to understand this guy — this idea of faith and action. But come on — wasn't it easy for him? I mean, he wrote books. Even that talk he gave at the Conference — I mean, his life wasn't in danger then or anything.

Activist 1: Let us show you something.

Activist 2: Now that you understand Dr. Heschel's background, let's skip ahead.

Activist 3: The year is 1965. The place is Selma, Alabama.

Activist 4: Dr. Martin Luther King, Jr. has organized a 12-day march from Selma to the capital of Alabama, Montgomery.

Narrator: Twelve days? Okay, I understand action, but isn't that extreme? Where did they sleep?

Activist 1: They slept in fields.

Activist 2: The first attempted march was stopped by the local police. They demanded that the protestors turn around. They used force and intimidation.

Activist 3: Many of the marchers were beaten.

Activist 4: Dr. King would not give up. He organized a second march two days later.

(Dr. King steps forward and addresses the audience.)

Dr. King: I can not promise you that you will not be beaten. I can not promise you that the police will not use force. But I can promise you that you are marching for a worthy cause — to protest the practices that keep Negro people from voting in Alabama!

Narrator: People were beaten two days ago, forced to turn around and march back . . . and he's telling people to try again?

Activist 1: This time, the Federal government supported us.

Activist 2: Civil rights became a national issue under Lyndon B. Johnson's administration.

Activist 3: Federal guards guaranteed that we could march safely, in peace.

Activist 4: It wasn't only the armed guards that made a difference this time, it was the emotional, spiritual, and physical presence of religious leaders from all over the country.

Activist 1: That's right. Clergy from all over the country came to Selma to march in support.

Narrator: Let me guess . . . Rabbi Heschel was there!

(Heschel enters and locks arm with Dr. King. They slowly march across the stage.)

Everyone sings: We shall overcome, we shall overcome.
We shall overcome some day.
Oh deep in my heart, I do believe
That we shall overcome some day.

Narrator: Dr. Heschel . . . Dr. Heschel . . . let me ask you something. I'm wondering, how does it feel . . . to be marching from Selma with Dr. King?

Heschel: I feel . . . I feel as if my legs are praying!

(Rabbi Heschel and Dr. King march off the stage. The Chorus follows them.)

Narrator: By marching from Selma . . . he felt his legs were praying! (*Pause.*) Prayer can be more than utterances from our lips, thoughts in our heads. Prayer can be taking action — doing!

(The Chorus enters.)

Activist 1: Prayer can be dance!

Activist 2: Prayer can be visiting the sick.

Activist 3: Prayer can be giving comfort.

Activist 4: Prayer can be standing up and speaking out for what we believe in.

Narrator: I think I understand now why the Civil Rights workers put their lives on the line — to change the world. I think I understand courage. I understand Rabbi Heschel's message — the message he wrote about and taught . . . the message that he lived in his life . . . in his arms and heart, and in his legs.

Activist 1: As Rabbi Heschel taught, faith demands action.

Activist 2: Being Jewish means being responsible.

Activist 3: For the Jewish people . . . and for the entire world.

Activist 4: We are all created in the divine image.

(The Narrator turns to the audience.)

Narrator: Rabbi Heschel was like the prophets of old. He spoke out. His message was not always popular, but that didn't matter to him. He spoke for what he believed in. I will try to do the same. (*Pause.*) What about you? Would you have marched from Selma and risked being beaten? Would you have risked your life to save a Jewish person if you were a gentile in Nazi Europe?

Activist 1: These are not easy questions you're posing.

Narrator: No, they're not easy, but our faith demands we tackle tough challenges. What about today? What injustices do you see in the world around you? Is life fair for all people? What will you do? When will you speak?

Activist 2: These are questions to answer now and . . . every day.

Activist 3: Sing with us, in memory of two great men.

Activist 4: Dr. Martin Luther King, Jr . . . and the modern Jewish prophet, Abraham Joshua Heschel.

(They lead the audience in "We Shall Overcome.")

Rabbi Abraham Joshua Heschel,
*Jewish theologian and philosopher,
was professor of Jewish Ethics and
Mysticism at the Jewish Theological
Seminary in New York City from
1945 until his death at age 65 in 1972. His prolific scholarship
helped to shape modern Jewish thought. His many books include*
The Sabbath, The Prophets, *and* Man's Quest for God.
*From the mid 1950s until the time of his death, Heschel
combined his scholarly and religious life with a firm
commitment to political activism. He advocated for fair housing,
care for the aged, and educational reform. He was at the forefront
of protests and demonstrations in the 1960s and 1970s intended
to secure equal rights for American Blacks and to end the U.S.
military intervention in Vietnam.*

Ida Kaminska:
A Star Endures

Characters*

Presenter
Ida Kaminska
Meir Melman
Hollywood lady
Hollywood Man
Esther Rachel Kaminska/Rivka
Abraham Kaminska
Regina/Ruth Kaminska
Yosef Kaminska/Addy Rosner
Shalom Asch/Minister of Culture/Polish Official

* One actor may play several parts as suggested, or
smaller parts can be divided among a larger cast.

Costumes

Have fun with the "Hollywood" look. The Eastern
European characters should have simple, modest
clothing. Ida can slip a dress or smock over her Oscar
dress when she goes back in time.

Props

A violin, some suitcases, and an envelope.

Setting

To portray Ida Kaminska's life on and off stage, create a
"stage" setting — a simple curtain on poles, some stage
lights. The stage looms as a presence, even when Ida is
"off stage." This effect could also be achieved with
lighting — be imaginative.

*(Ida and Meir sit in the audience at the Academy Award
ceremony, 1966 —facing out at the real audience —waiting for
the big moment. Near them are two "Hollywood types" loudly
giving their opinions, as the Presenter announces the nominees.)*

Presenter: Thank you, ladies and gentleman! It is truly
an honor to be here tonight to announce the nominees
for Best Actress in a leading role. The members of the
Academy have selected five outstanding actresses. And
the nominees are:

Hollywood Lady: It's the same list every year. The
Academy always has their favorites.

Hollywood man: Don't be bitter, darling. You'll be
nominated one year. "Doris and the Monkey from Mars"
was your best work, and it can only get better from here
on!

Presenter: This year, we have a unique situation. Two
nominees from the same family! Both Lynn Redgrave and
her sister Vanessa Redgrave are nominees for Best Actress
in a leading role!

Hollywood Lady: Those Redgraves! Really! Who do they
think they are?

Hollywood Man: They are from one of Britain's most
famous theater families, muffin-pie. You can't deny them
their heritage.

Hollywood Lady: Then they should go back to England!
These are American awards!

Presenter: Besides the Redgrave sisters, there is Anouk
Aimee, one of France's most romantic actresses.

Meir: Are you getting nervous, Ida?

Ida: Please, Meir, in our lives, we have had many things to be nervous about. Winning an award is not one of them.

Presenter: And of course, the next nominee is America's own sweetheart, the most beautiful woman in the world — Elizabeth Taylor!

Hollywood Lady: Baloney! She's not so beautiful! Right, scrumptious? Right?

Hollywood Man: Did . . . uh, did you say something, cupcake? I was watching the clip of Elizabeth Taylor. She really is the most beautiful woman in the world!

Hollywood Lady: Oh! You can find your own ride home tonight!

Meir: I wish they'd be quiet. The big moment is coming.

Ida: It's all right, Meir. It will all be over soon.

Presenter: Our next nominee is less familiar to American audiences. Yet, she wowed the Academy with her performance in "The Shop on Main Street," in which she played a Jewish shopkeeper in Poland during the Nazis occupation. I am pleased to announce the Academy's nomination of Ida Kaminska, the grande dame of Yiddish Theater!

Hollywood Lady: (*Standing up.*) Ida Kaminska! Ida Kaminska! Who on God's green earth is that? I was overlooked by the Academy . . . for Ida Kaminska?

Hollywood Man: You weren't overlooked, poo-poo. It was the film. The critics always prefer movies like "The

Shop on Main Street" to "Doris and the Monkey from Mars"!

Hollywood Lady: You shut up! Shut up! You're still in the doghouse!

Hollywood Man: Well, since the doghouse is carpeted, heated, and has its own Jacuzzi . . . it could be worse.

Meir: I can't stand it anymore! Those obnoxious Hollywood types! I want to show the world who you are. I want them to see the real Ida Kaminska.

Ida: Meir, please. It's the middle of the awards ceremony.

Meir: So what? Just imagine . . . imagine all we could tell them about you, Ida, and about your life on and off the stage!

(Meir stands. He takes Ida by the hand and guides her to center stage. The other people exit, and stagehands remove the chairs.)

Meir: You all know, of course, what is Yiddish Theater? No? Well, let me tell you this much. Yiddish Theater began in Eastern Europe, in the eighteenth century, during the Age of Enlightenment, when many left the study of religion to study secular subjects. People began studying philosophy, science . . . even theater! But the Jewish people were still connected to their culture. So, they wrote plays in Yiddish, and soon, Yiddish Theater troupes sprang up all over Europe, entertaining every kind of Jew out there — from the very religious to the ultra-secular. Everyone enjoyed the Yiddish Theater . . . especially in Warsaw, at the turn of the twentieth century, when the most popular, most acclaimed actors were the legendary Kaminska family!

(In the "stage area," Ida is joined by her mother, Esther Rachel Kaminska.)

Esther Rachel: Ida-leh?

Ida: Yes, Mama?

Esther Rachel: Would you like to be in a play?

Ida: A play?

Esther Rachel: I need a little child to play my granddaughter in "The Mother." I think my little Ida would be perfect! You are almost five years old. You're not a baby anymore.

Ida: What about Regina, Mama? She always plays the little child.

Esther Rachel: Your older sister can't be in plays for now. Your father and I have decided that she should get an education. You will go to school, too, when you get older. My daughters should have an education, just like your brother Yosef.

Ida: I don't need to go to school, Mama. I want to be a famous actress like you!

Esther Rachel: The theater is a hard life, Ida. You see that already. Papa and I are always touring. If your aunt didn't take care of you children when we were gone, what would we do? We depend on the box office to make a living. The audience is fickle. Sometimes they like one kind of show and sometimes another. There were times, Ida, when your Papa and I only had one sour pickle to share between us. That's how poor we were.

Ida: But now we live in a nice house in Warsaw! We have lots of food.

Esther Rachel: Times are good. I've just been invited to Paris, and then to America, to perform in the Yiddish Theater.

Ida: But first, we will perform "The Mother" here?

Esther Rachel: Yes, my little actress. It will be your debut!

(Lights down on the stage and up on Meir.)

Meir: Times were good for the Kaminska family in Poland before the World Wars. Ida and her sister Regina and brother Yosef went to school, but they always had one foot in the theater. The Kaminska home was a kind of salon, which all the great Yiddish writers and artists would visit.

(Lights back on the stage. The Kaminska family sits together, drinking tea. A knock is heard at the door.)

Ida: I'll get it! (*She goes to the door. It is the great writer, Sholem Asch.*) Mr. Asch, please come in!

Asch: Thank you, Ida. You look very beautiful today.

Ida: Thank you. We were just having tea.

Abraham: (*Getting up, to shake Asch's hand.*) Come join us, Sholem. We were just in the midst of a heated debate — nothing unusual for the Kaminska family!

Esther Rachel: Talk some sense into my husband, Sholem. He has such crazy ideas sometimes!

Abraham: What's crazy? Listen, Sholem, we have some money. Mama just came back from touring in Paris. I'm tired of renting. I want to buy a space for our theater troupe.

Asch: Nothing wrong with that!

Regina: Now comes the crazy part.

Abraham: I saw a great little theater, just perfect for us. Only . . . it's not in the Jewish neighborhood. So what? Why can't we mix with the Polish people? More and more assimilated Jews are moving out of this neighborhood. The Polish people should see that we're just like them. We don't need to live in a ghetto. These are modern times. Who knows, maybe they'll even come to our theater.

Asch: You're taking a risk, Abraham. I can't imagine a non-Jewish neighborhood would welcome Jews, let alone a Jewish Theater.

Ida: I don't understand. Why do they hate us? Why do they hate us, just for being Jewish?

(Everyone is quiet.)

Esther Rachel: Some things are hard to understand, Ida-leh. Even for your parents.

Yosef: I hear the Polish boys in the park. They yell at the old Jewish men who sit there reading the paper. They yell, "Go back to Palestine!"

Abraham: If they knew us, if we mixed, they couldn't hate us so much.

Esther Rachel: My crazy husband. What can I do?

Asch: I can always count on a heated discussion in the Kaminska house. That's why I love to come here! But enough talk. We can't solve these problems today. I also come here for the great music. Yosef, you young maestro, play the violin!

(Yosef "plays" to a recording of Mozart. Lights go down on the stage. Ida steps out of the stage, toward Meir.)

Ida: Meir, we can't explain my entire life story! That would bore the audience.

Meir: Ida, my dear, your life has been many things, but never boring!

Ida: So, I grew up and acted in and directed many plays. Let's skip ahead to the war, at least.

Meir: As you wish. (*Pause, as Ida goes back to the stage.*) We skip ahead now. Ida is no longer a child, but an adult, a mother herself. It is 1939. Ida has lost her dear parents, and also her sister Regina. Brother Yosef is living in Palestine. Ida has also had a full, happy life, taking her mother's place as the grande dame of Yiddish Theater. Ida played to packed houses all over Eastern Europe, with her innovative productions and Yiddish translations of the greatest plays of the time. Ida's daughter, Ruth, was following in her mother and grandmother's footsteps to become an actress. And what else? Ah, yes, Ida and I met in the theater . . . and fell in love. It was, as I said, a very good life. (*Pause.*) We thought it would go on that way. But you know the Yiddish saying, "Man plans and God laughs." Look now. It's August, 1939.

(Meir steps into the stage. Ida sits with Ruth and her husband, Addy.)

Addy: This war is not helping my career. That is for certain. Last night, not a single soul came to the café! No one cares about jazz music anymore.

Ruth: It will pass soon, Addy. It has nothing to do with your music, dear. People are just afraid to leave their homes. They think any day — any day the Nazis will come here, to Poland! *(Pause.)* After the war is over, people will come hear you play again.

Addy: I just want to be a good husband, Ruth. Money is so scarce. I don't know how we'll get through this difficult period.

Ida: Don't you worry, Addy. The Kaminska family sticks together . . . and we always pull through!

Meir: *(Playing with a radio.)* Dammit! I can't get the BBC at all! Tonight it's crucial that we find out what's going on in the world!

Ida: Try Radio Moscow, at least.

Meir: All I can get is the Third Reich. Listen!

(A recording of a Nazi officer.)

Nazi Officer: Germany has officially attacked Poland. Poland will fall soon! Today is the first day of the Third Reich, the new Nazi era, which shall last for a thousand years!

(All are silent for a moment.)

Ida: What do we do now? And what does the BBC report — all the terrible things that are happening to the Jews.

Meir: I've been studying the maps. I have an escape plan.

Ruth: Do we have to leave Poland? All our family is here, our friends . . .

Addy: It won't be for long, darling.

Meir: Ida, Ruth, start packing. Take your warmest clothes. Only what you can carry.

Ruth: But all our albums — the pictures and the programs from Mama's shows . . . and Grandmama's . . .

Ida: We won't be gone long, Ruth. We'll come back. Everything will be safe here.

(Suddenly, the sound of bombing is heard. The family freezes.)

Addy: My God! Look outside — all the buildings — have collapsed — in the street. People are dying!

Meir: Let's go, now. We'll find a shelter! We need to be underground, where the bombs can't reach us. Leave everything! Come now, come!

Ida: But we have no food, Meir, we have no . . .

Meir: We have our lives, Ida. That's more than many right now.

Ida: This feels like a movie I've seen, a play I've starred in. This can't be real! This can't be happening to us!

Ruth: We are together, Mama. Just like in the theater. We will survive this, Mama.

Meir: When we get outside, follow in a line, single file. Stay close — ready?

(They all exit, Ida remains alone for a moment.)

Ida: Good-bye, my theater. Good-bye, my home.

(She exits. Meir steps forward.)

Meir: What's in the next scene? I couldn't possible re-create it, even with the finest actors on the grandest stage. (*Pause.*) We made it to a shelter. It was so packed with people you couldn't turn your shoulders — old people, children, babies. Some had been injured in the bombings. No food, no water. In a few days, it would be Yom Kippur — the Day of Atonement. We all fasted, not only in penitence, but also simply because there was nothing to eat. We prayed, not with words from our tradition — there were no prayer books, no Hazzan — we prayed with our tears, with our sobs, our moans. (*Pause.*) I had a plan for our escape. We would hire a driver to take us to the border of the Soviet Union. I believed we would be free there — the land where everyone was equal. How did we make it there safely? How did anyone escape? A little mazel, a little chutzpah . . . and a whole lot of faith. It didn't hurt that we spoke fluent German, and people were anxious to help us, the famous actors. We made our escape.

(Lights up on stage. Ida, Ruth, and Addy have a few small bags with them.)

Ruth: Where are we? I feel like we've been on the train for days!

Ida: We're very far to the east, Ruth, near Siberia. Go back to sleep, now. Meir went to see if we can stop here.

Addy: This is nonsense! They won't give us a permit to come into town, but we have nowhere else to go. The Soviets are too much! They should be honored to have us. They've never seen culture like when we perform!

Ruth: Maybe we should have stayed in Baku. Why did we have to travel so deep into Asia?

Ida: You heard the rumors there, darling. The Germans were coming closer. Besides, the Nazis started to brainwash the Russians that they had taken prisoner.

Ruth: I heard them in the market place. The wounded Russian soldiers were saying, "It's the fault of the Jews . . . they started it all."

Ida: Better we are deep in Asia, where people haven't heard the German propaganda yet.

(Meir enters. With him is Rivka, one of Ida's old theater friends.)

Meir: Good news! The town of Frunze will give us permits! And not only that, we have friends here! Friends from Warsaw!

Ida: Rivka, is it you? Imagine meeting almost in Siberia!

Rivka: It's a miracle! There are others, too — writers and artists. You'll all feel at home. Many Jewish refugees have come here.

Ida: It's settled then. We must start a theater. A Yiddish Theater in Frunze!

Meir: Ida, Ida . . . let's first find lodging . . . and food. You and Ruth need to rest.

Ida: Meir, you know more than anyone, I am not alive if I'm not making plays. And besides, the refugees . . . think how it will help them, half way across the world to hear the *mama-loshen*, the mother tongue. Think how more now than ever, we need tragedies to cry with. Meir, we need comedies to cheer us.

Rivka: Come, everyone, I can help you find a hotel. There's more food in the markets here than there is in the west. You can rest and eat . . . and Ida, in no time, you will start your Yiddish Theater . . .

Meir: You are unstoppable, Ida. I suppose that's why I love you.

Ruth: A hotel! A clean bed! A bath! I can't even remember these simple things. It's been so long.

(Rivka leads them offstage.)

Meir: We stayed in the town of Frunze for two years. Of course, Ida started her Yiddish Theater and we all performed in it. The refugees came to all the plays, as did some of the natives . . . who couldn't understand a word of Yiddish. We were lucky to be in Frunze. Of course, we tried to get the BBC on the radio, so we could hear about our friends, our family in Poland . . . who weren't as lucky as we. (*Pause.*) The poison of anti-Semitism . . . started to reach us in Frunze. Even in Central Asia, people started to hate the Jews. We had to leave. Next stop: Moscow!

(Ida is onstage alone.)

Ida: I've been in Moscow for almost two years now, but never once invited to perform! Everything must be approved by the Soviet government . . . even who gets to stand upon the stage. It's taken all this time just to get an appointment with the Minister of Cultural affairs. And now, he's nearly an hour late!

(The Minister of Cultural Affairs enters.)

Minister: Let me see your portfolio . . . your pictures and reviews . . .

Ida: Here is all the work I've done in Russia . . . er, the Soviet Union. I had to leave all my other reviews in Poland when we fled. I was known there as the greatest actress in the Yiddish Theater.

Minister: Yes. We know who you are.

Ida: I've been in Moscow nearly two years, but I've never been invited to perform . . .

Minister: The All-Russian Theater Society will permit you to perform here . . . for one night.

Ida: Thank you. Thank you so much for this opportunity, sir! When I don't perform, I feel as though I'm not alive. I don't think you'll be disappointed!

Minister: Of course, you will give your performance tonight in Polish.

Ida: In Polish! But I am known through the world as a Yiddish actress! I perform only in Yiddish.

Minister: I am a busy man, Miss Kaminska. Take your portfolio. You may go.

Ida: There will be no performance then?

Minister: Ours is not a Yiddish Theater, Miss Kaminska. We don't need your "special" skills.

Ida: When the Soviet Union bans Yiddish Theater, it is making a grave mistake! Thank you for your graciousness! Good day, sir.

(Ida exits dramatically. Lights down on the stage.)

Meir: While we were living in Moscow, I had a job with Soviet radio as an announcer. I got to see the news releases before anyone else! On May 7, 1945, I called Ida.

Ida: *(Entering the stage.)* Hello?

Meir: Ida, it's me!

Ida: Hello, darling. Aren't you at work?

Meir: Yes, that's why I'm calling. You must listen to the news at eleven o'clock.

Ida: I'm tired, darling, and the news is so depressing.

Meir: Just listen. Trust me. I can't tell you what the news is now. It's classified information. But you will want to hear it.

Ida: All right, all right. My radio is on.

Meir: At eleven o'clock, I announced: The Germans have finally been defeated and a cease-fire agreement has been reached!

Ida: At last, at last! The Nazis are no more. We can finally . . . finally go HOME!

Meir: Now some of you may find it strange that Ida and I were so anxious to return to Poland . . . after the Nazis had nearly destroyed all of Jewish culture there. But that's exactly why we wanted to go — so we could re-build what had been lost, so the Nazis wouldn't be victors, so our beloved Yiddish theater could rise again. (*Pause.*) We obtained our passports to leave rather quickly. Ruth and Addy were on tour and said they'd join us later. When we entered Poland, we were not prepared for what we saw . . .

Ida: Meir, Meir! These ruins! They are like visions that can only be imagines in nightmares! Buildings bombed, destroyed. Twisted steel and stone. Were these our homes? Our theater? And this? This was the famous Warsaw ghetto — where our friends and family risked their lives to fight the Nazis, to fight for freedom. Now all has been reduced to rubble and dust and sand and stone. The Jewish cemeteries — nearly all destroyed. Only this one remains — with my Mother's grave. Oh Mama, you would not believe what has happened to your precious Warsaw. You could not imagine that the city where you were so beloved could treat its Jews this way.

Meir: Enough, Ida. Let's go now.

Ida: (*Pause.*) We must rebuild, Meir. We must give the Jews who remain here — the survivors — we must give them back their lives. Remind them that they are human beings who can laugh and hope and cry. We must make a theater for them. I don't know how we'll do it, but do it we shall. I believe we can, Meir, I believe . . .

(*Lights down on Ida.*)

Meir: You know my Ida, by now. We made a theater!

(Lights onstage, Ida meets with Polish official.)

Ida: And you see, if we receive state funding, I can be the Artistic Director of the new Yiddish Theater and my husband Meir can be the Administrative Director. He's just wonderful with administrative details and he's a great actor, as you know.

Polish Official: Miss Kaminska, in terms of the permit, there should be no problem. There is just . . . one thing . . . I want to make clear . . .

Ida: Yes?

Official: Poland is not the Soviet Union. We have no Stalin here.

Ida: That's why we left Moscow. He was starting to hunt down the Jewish intellectuals and artists . . .

Official: That is not our policy here, you understand?

Ida: I was eager to come back to Warsaw.

Official: During the war, the Jews of Poland were all but liquidated. *(Pause.)* There may be some — in the government — who do not regret this unfortunate matter.

Ida: I see.

Official: I am not among them. I am going to sign the documents to give you your Yiddish State Theater. *(Pause.)* But I thought you should know this.

Ida: Thank you for the permit . . . and for your . . . support.

(Ida shakes his hand and exits. The Official follows.)

Meir: In fact, our Yiddish State Theater was popular among Poland's Jewish audience and among many non-Jews. Not only were we thriving in post-war Poland, but also around the world! Ida and I began to tour.

(Ida appears on stage with her valise.)

Meir: First stop, Paris!

Ida: Paris, France! I remember when Mama performed here!

Meir: London!

Ida: Who was in the audience tonight? The Queen? And she wants to meet me? Please, send her backstage!

Meir: Australia!

Ida: I've never seen . . . a landscape like this!

Meir: Perhaps most important, Israel!

Ida: Oh, Meir, such beauty in this young country, and such strength in the hands and hearts of those who build it. Some here have suffered so much. And to receive such a warm welcome! Oh Meir, we could come here and set up a home . . . should anything happen in Poland.

Meir: Should we leave Warsaw? Should we stay?

Ida: I think the Jews in Warsaw need us more now . . .

Meir: I agree. We stayed in Poland. (*Pause.*) And our theater thrived and helped the Jewish community find its strength and spirit again.

Ida: Oh, and tell them about the film.

Meir: I thought that wasn't so important.

Ida: The award is not important, but the film is significant!

Meir: Then you tell them, darling!

Ida: In Poland, there was still hostility against the Jews and I was never once cast in a Polish film. But in 1964, two Czechoslovakian directors, Jan Kader and Elmar Klos, selected me for a role in "The Shop on Main Street." The film has an outspoken Jewish theme and went on to worldwide success. Which brings me here, to Hollywood, to the Academy Awards!

Meir: I, for one, would like to see who wins. Shall we be seated?

Ida: Of course! You were the one, Meir, who wanted to tell this little tale.

(The two of them return to their original seats, as does the Hollywood couple. The Presenter returns to the stage.)

Presenter: And the envelope, please! The winner of the Oscar for Best Actress goes to Elizabeth Taylor for "Who's Afraid of Virginia Woolf"!

Hollywood Lady: It figures! Liz Taylor! I hope she gets really, really fat some day!

Hollywood Man: What, darling? Did you say something?

Meir: I'm sorry, Ida.

Ida: Thank you, Meir. But I am not sorry. I am honored to be here tonight. And I am thankful, to God, that we have survived . . . and lived our dream.

Meir: Amen.

(Lights down.)

After many years of creating theater in Eastern Europe, **Ida Kaminska** *and her husband Meir Melman settled in the United States in 1968. Her autobiography,* My Life, My Theater, *was published in English in 1973. In 1974, disappointed in her attempts to establish a Yiddish repertory theater in the United States, Ida and Meir decided to move to Israel. They joined a short-lived Yiddish theater in Tel Aviv. A few years later, they returned to the U.S. Ida died in New York in 1980, at age 81. She is remembered and cherished in the theater world for her lifelong contributions to the Yiddish Theater.*

Aaron Lansky:
A Modern Pakn Treger[1]

Characters

Aaron
Mother
Father
Yiddish Muse
Old Man 1
Old Man 2
Old Man 3
Rabbi
Friend 1
Friend 2
Friend 3
Professor Piccus
Professor Ruth Wisse
Mr. Spiegelman
Philanthropist
Reporter
Book helpers

Setting

Basic tables and chairs can easily be used to construct the
various settings: synagogue, university, people's homes,
etc. If the play is being produced in a more elaborate
fashion, a backdrop painted with an Eastern European
shtetl could help convey the imagery of Yiddish culture.

Props

Essential props: stacks of books and a telephone. Other
props may be added as desired to enhance each scene.

---

[1] The original *pakn tregers* traveled from *shetl* to *shetl* in Eastern Europe bringing books
and news of the outside world.

Costumes

While most of these characters are contemporary, the Muse is set apart in time. She might wear clothes from the last century, or even some form of "angel" wings or other magical garb. Be creative with her and allow the Muse to emerge!

Yiddish

Try and find someone who speaks Yiddish who can serve as a dialogue coach and help with pronunciation. You may just become inspired to learn Yiddish yourself!

Scene 1. At the synagogue.

(Aaron, ten years old, is entering the synagogue with his Father and Mother.)

Aaron: Do we really have to go to synagogue tonight? Can't we turn around and go home?

Mother: Aaron, it's a holiday. You know that.

Father: You don't have it bad, Aaron. When I was kid, my Father dragged me to services all the time. We only make you go on major holidays.

Mother: And Shabbat, sometimes. It's important to go and learn about your religion.

Aaron: But people go and sit in the front of the sanctuary . . . and act so religious. But they aren't that way outside of the synagogue . . . most people don't even keep kosher.

Father: Hey — it's America, Aaron. We're not back in the old country.

Mother: Which doesn't mean we shouldn't go to services. So once in a while, would it hurt you to learn a few prayers?

Aaron: I guess not. I just wish it weren't so . . . so boring.

(The Muse enters with a flourish. No one on stage sees her, but Aaron can half hear her.)

Muse: Boring, *boychick*? *Ich'l dir gebn an eytse* — I'll give you a suggestion.

Aaron: Huh? What was that?

Muse: *Boychick, Ich'l dir gebn an eytse.*

Aaron: I don't understand.

Mother: Well, now's not the time to discuss it. We're already late — how embarrassing. Let's walk in quietly.

Aaron: I thought I . . . I thought I . . . heard something just then —

Muse: Ahhh, *boychick, de mame loshen*[2], you don't know so good yet. I'll try it in American. It means *Boychick*, I'll give you a suggestion.

Aaron: Suggestion?

Father: Aaron, a suggestion we don't need right now! Listen to your Mother. Be quiet as we go in.

---

2 The mother tongue.

Aaron: Yeah, Dad — okay.

Muse: *Deigheh nisht* — don't worry! They don't hear me. But you Aaron, listen close: I'll tell you how to make these services more exciting. The Rabbi, *Baruch Hashem*, thanks be to God, is a nice man. But what you should listen to . . . if you really want to hear something exciting . . . listen to the *alter kockers*, the old guys, in the back. From them, you could learn a *bisl mame loshen*.

(The Muse exits.)

Aaron: Can we sit in the back at least . . . where the old men sit?

Mother: We'll have to tonight. It's almost time for the "Barchu."

(Aaron, Mother, and Father "enter" the synagogue. At the front stands the Rabbi, going through the motions of a service. In the back rows are the old men. Aaron and his parents sit just in front of them.)

Old Man 1: *A Groyser Oylem, un nito keyn mentsh!*[3]

Old Man 2: *Di gantse velt iz mishugge!*[4]

Aaron: Dad, what are they saying?

Father: Who?

Aaron: The old guys back there. You know Yiddish. What are they talking about?

---

3 In the whole world, not one righteous man!
4 The whole world is crazy!
5 You'll be the death of me!

114

Father: Who knows? Try and follow along with the Rabbi. You're going to become a Bar Mitzvah soon. You gotta learn how the service goes.

Old Man 3: *Oy, Du fatkirtst mir di yoren!*[5]

Aaron: Dad, what are they drinking? What do they have in those water glasses?

Father: I don't know . . . whiskey, I guess. You know, Shnapps. What's with the questions? When did these guys become so interesting?

Aaron: I don't know . . . there's just something I like about . . . the way they talk. They have so much soul. The rest of us just sit here and try and follow the Rabbi. I wish I could sit with them and understand them.

Father: They talk Yiddish, they drink Shnapps . . . they're leftovers from the Old World. This is America. We're past the middle of the twentieth century. We don't have those old ways . . . we're modern, American Jews.

Aaron: I know, Dad. I know.

Old Man 1: *Eyn velt, un aleh chayes!*[6]

Rabbi: Please join with me for our concluding song.

(The Congregation sings "Adon Olam." The Muse appears and "blesses" Aaron by putting her hands over his head, as with the ancient priestly blessing. He does not "see" her. At the end of the song, everyone exits.)

---

6 One world, with all these animals! (The Old Man is commenting on the "modern" Jews, like Aaron and his family. He assumes no one can understand him.)

Scene 2. Aaron's college dorm room.

(Aaron is now a freshman in college. He is hanging out with his friend.)

Friend: So have you heard about any good parties this weekend?

Aaron: There's always something going on.

Friend: Man, I'm so glad I chose Hampshire. I have no idea what I want to study. I'm taking a little of this, doing a little of that.

Aaron: Yeah, I don't know, either. I can't even imagine what I'm going to do with the rest of my life. I have one class I'm really into. That's all I know.

Friend: Yeah? What's that?

Aaron: It's this class — on the Holocaust.

Friend: Oh. Heavy.

Aaron: Yeah. But you know . . . I realize . . . I'm not that interested in the Holocaust itself . . . I mean, the mechanics of how it happened. That's what the class is about. But it's got me thinking . . . what was Jewish life like in Europe before the Nazis came to power? I mean, what was it about the Jews that the Nazis wanted to destroy so badly?

Friend: The Nazis were fascists. They didn't want anyone around who would challenge their power.

Aaron: Exactly! See — it just makes me think — Jewish culture must have been the opposite of fascist . . . there must have been something going on . . . that was creative and democratic . . . and counterculture . . .

Friend: Counterculture? Come on, Aaron. I don't think being Jewish is what you'd call counterculture.

Aaron: I'm not talking about what we have here in America . . . at our suburban synagogues. I want to find out what life was like in Europe, before the Nazis came to power. I just have this feeling . . . it's so strange . . . it's as if I was compelled to take this class on the Holocaust . . . and as if I'm compelled to find out about Jewish culture. This is totally crazy, but ever since I was a kid, I wanted so badly to understand Yiddish . . .

Friend: Yiddish? What, do you want to work in the Catskills as a comic after you graduate? Is there any money in that?

(Muse enters and responds to the conversation.)

Muse: *Oy, oy, oy! A cham mit bilding iz nit mer vi a gebildte cham.*[7]

(Aaron starts laughing.)

Friend: Well? What's so funny?

Aaron: I don't know . . . I'm sorry . . . sometimes, I think I hear things . . . and they're usually pretty funny!

Friend: Aaron, you didn't start partying without me did you? It's only Wednesday night.

Aaron: No, no. I swear, I'm just tired. Too much studying.

---

7 A dope with an education is just an educated dope.

Friend: Yeah — lighten up a little. It's only college.

Aaron: Yeah — yeah. You're right. Only college.

(*Friend exits.*)

Aaron: *A cham mit bilding iz nit mer vi a gebildte cham!* A dope with an education is just an educated dope!

(*Aaron and the Muse laugh together. Aaron takes his backpack and exits. The Muse follows him.*)

Scene 3. Professor Piccus's study.

(*Professor Piccus is snoozing. Aaron knocks and walks in.*)

Aaron: Professor Piccus? Excuse me, am I in the right place?

Piccus: (*Waking up.*) Vas — vas — who is it?

Aaron: It's me . . . Aaron. Aaron Lansky. I spoke with you on the phone . . .

Piccus: Oy, the one who wants to learn *de mama loshen* . . .

Aaron: Yiddish, I want to learn Yiddish. I've been learning, studying about life in Europe before the Holocaust and I just have this feeling . . . that for me to really understand life there, I . . . should know the language, I should read the books . . .

Piccus: Good, so we'll begin.

Aaron: Begin?

Piccus: Begin reading. Yiddish. That's what you want to do, yes?

Aaron: Yes, but . . . I mean . . . I don't know anything.

Piccus: You brought the wine? Let's open.

Aaron: Yes, like you asked . . . a bottle of wine . . . oh, and bread, I brought you this good bread!

Piccus: So . . . you're learning already!

Aaron: I . . . I realize how valueable your time is . . . a professor of medieval history . . . I would be happy to pay you . . . not that I have money or anything . . .

Piccus: So you'll bring a bottle of wine and we'll drink and we'll read *de mama loshen*. Let's begin.

Aaron: Begin — right. Professor Piccus, I don't know any Yiddish.

Piccus: There's no shame in that — you're here to learn. *Boychick*, you know how many languages I speak?

Aaron: I don't know. Three, maybe four?

Piccus: Twenty! But Yiddish — *de mama loshen* — that's the one I learned first. From a child in my Mama's arms. (*Pause.*) So I think I can teach you. We just need to begin. Let's start with Singer. (*He hands Aaron a book*). Open it up.

Aaron: Isaac Bashevis Singer?

Piccus: You never heard of him? No matter. His stories. I think you'll like. You'll read. I'll translate. We'll study grammar, conjugate verbs. In no time, *Yungerman*, you'll speak it. Yiddish. Easy as . . . a glass of wine. Here. Take a sip. Relax. Now read. Read to me.

(The Muse enters. She pours herself a glass of wine and looks over Aaron's shoulder.)

Muse: *The Brothers Askenaz*, one of my favorite novels! *Es gefelt mir*, I like it, *boychick*! You learning *de mama loshen*. I have great plans for you! Look at my Aaronalah . . . *Braiter vi lainger* — oy, he's so happy!

Piccus: *Gut, gut* . . . go on . . .

(He winks at the Muse. Lights down.)

Scene 4. Graduation day.

(Aaron and a group of friends (guys and girls) are dressed in caps and gowns. It is moments before their graduation ceremony.)

Friend 1: I can't believe it! Four years just flew by like no time. It seems impossible that we're graduating today.

Friend 2: We have to believe it — we're going to walk down that aisle any second and get our diplomas. Our carefree college days are behind us.

Friend 3: Only if you let them be. I'm going to stick around Amherst and get a job.

Friend 1: Doing what?

Friend 3: Whatever . . . maybe washing dishes or something. I just want to chill. I just finished four years of studying!

Friend 2: Like you ever studied!

Friend 3: I did . . . sometimes . . .

Friend 2: I have two weeks off, then I start clerking in my Dad's law firm, and then I start law school in September.

Friend 1: Law school? But all through college you were talking like you were so anti-establishment!

Friend 2: Grow up and smell the coffee! It's easy to talk that way in college. But in the real world . . . money talks. I may go into corporate law. Who knows. So what are you going to do that's so remarkable?

Friend 1: No problem — I've been accepted to three medical schools. What about you, Aaron?

Aaron: Oh . . . I just got word. I've been accepted in a Ph.D. program at McGill University in Montreal.

Friend 3: Hey, congrats, Aaron! So you'll be a doctor, too!

Friend 2: A doctor in what? What will you be studying?

Aaron: Uh . . . you know . . . actually Eastern European Jewish Studies.

Friend 1: Wow, Aaron. You've turned religious. Are you going to become a Rabbi?

Aaron: No . . . no . . . I'm not really religious . . . I mean, I am, I feel very connected to this stuff . . . but it's not like in a traditional religious way.

Friend 2: I have a cousin who turned religious. She changed her name and is married to a meat cutter in Crown Heights. She's 25 and has six children. I'd watch out, Aaron.

Aaron: This is . . . an intellectual path. Since I started studying Yiddish with Professor Piccus . . . well, even before that . . . I've always had this desire . . . to learn about life in Europe . . . to understand what it was like.

Friend 1: So what are you going to do with this, once you have your Ph.D.?

Aaron: I guess I'll . . . I'll probably teach.

Friend 3: Do other people care — I mean, do other people want to learn this . . . Yiddish stuff?

Aaron: *Drey Zich nit keyn kop mit —*

Friends: Huh?

Aaron: You shouldn't bother your head with it. I'll be fine!

Friend 1: Oh . . . listen, guys, it's "Pomp and Circumstance" . . . come on, let's get in line.

(The Muse follows after them and turns to the audience.)

Muse: *(Wiping her eyes with a handkerchief.)* My little *boychick* . . . growing up!

(All exit. Lights down.)

Scene 5. One year later.

(Aaron enters the office of his professor, Dr. Ruth Wisse.)

Dr. Wisse: Aaron, come in. I've been waiting for you.

Aaron: Sorry I'm late for our meeting . . . I was just trying to finish some reading. There's always so much reading to do.

Dr. Wisse: Welcome to graduate school! (*Pause.*) You've been here at McGill for nearly a year now. Nu? How do you think it's going?

Aaron: School? I love it! I feel like I'm learning so much from you, Dr. Wisse. I feel so privleged to study with you.

Dr. Wisse: You have an eager mind, Aaron. What's more, I know how much your studies mean to you. How much you care about the subject matter.

Aaron: I've often felt . . . such an incredible attraction to Yiddish culture. Not in a nostalgic way, like we should go back to Europe or live in the past. It's that I think Yiddish culture would help American Jews gain a better understanding of who we are . . .

Dr. Wisse: That's why I assign you extra books, Aaron. If you want to know the culture, you must become steeped in it. You must read. Literature holds the real key to a people's heart, their soul.

Aaron: You've given me quite a list . . . this semester and for my summer reading. I want to read these books. The problem is, I can't find them. The library here at McGill only has a few Yiddish books. I tried the book dealers you suggested — nothing. It seems like all the great Yiddish works have disappeared.

Dr. Wisse: I can't believe that, Aaron. People treated these books like their *kinder* — their children . . . they loved and protected them. They packed them in their bags when they left the Old Country. They must be out there. You're just not looking in the right places.

Aaron: What do you suggest? Where should I look?

Dr. Wisse: You're a creative young man, Aaron. You'll figure it out. Now, if you'll excuse me, I'm late for a faculty meeting. Let's check in again, later in the summer. I really must go —

Aaron: Dr. Wisse . . .

Dr. Wisse: Yes, Aaron?

Aaron: Thank you. And, *zi gezunt*.[8]

(She smiles and exits. Aaron sits for a few moments, puzzled. He stands and begins to pace. The Muse enters.)

Muse: *Boychick*, your famous professor — she's right. The books written in *de mama loshen* are out there. You've got to figure a way to find them, to save them. You're on your own, Aaronalah. I — the Muse of Yiddish — have done my job. I have captured your imagination. But now, my Aaron, you must complete the task. Or try at least. As they say in *Pirke Avos:* You might not finish the job, but neither can you ignore it.

(Aaron sits quietly for a moment.)

---

8 Go in health.

Aaron: I could start here . . . in Montreal. I'll put signs up . . . where the old Jews go, the deli, the laundromat. "Graduate student seeking Yiddish Books!" It'll be easy, right? I can find the books I need to read this summer. I mean, I certainly can't find . . . I can't save . . . all the Yiddish books in the world! That's crazy. (*Pause.*) Why am I going through all of this *mishegas*[9]? I must have been given pickle juice in my bottle when I was a baby!

Muse: Call it what you will Aaron, but one thing you should know. These books will call you. They will find you. You can't turn back.

(*Aaron looks right at the Muse, as if seeing her for the first time.*)

Aaron: I can't turn back.

(*Aaron and the Muse exit at opposite sides of the stage.*)

Scene 6. Aaron's apartment.

(*Aaron is on the phone.*)

Aaron: Yeah, Ma . . . Yiddish books. No, anything, any subject. Right. Ask the Rabbi, at least. He might have some or know someone. Yeah, I just put up a few signs . . . and I'm getting calls. It's great! What am I going to do with them? I don't know . . . read them. Well, no not this summer . . . not all of them. Huh? Well, they should be in a library somewhere, I guess. Which library? Ma, I don't know — whoever wants them! Uh huh. Uh huh. Okay, thanks, Ma. Okay. Bye.

(*He hangs up. The phone rings as soon as he puts it down.*)

---

9 Craziness.

Aaron: Hello? Yes? Yes . . . I'm the one who put up the sign. Yes. You do? How many? Sholom Asch, I.L. Peretz, Shalom Aleichem. Those are classic books! Your kids don't want them? I see. I see. They don't speak Yiddish. I understand. No, yes, I mean . . . yes, I want them. Pick them up? Sure . . . what's your address? Great, I'll be right there. Thank you. Thank you. Good-bye.

(He hangs up. Phone rings again.)

Aaron: Hello? Yes, Rabbi? How are you? Good, good. Yes, I like school very much. What, my Mother called you? Yes, she works fast. Uh-huh. Uh-huh. A whole stack of Yiddish books? Right there? In your office? You were going to what? To bury them? But that's what you do with religious books — books that invoke God's name. Yes, yes, I understand. But Rabbi, these are secular books. No, please, don't bury them! I want them! They're . . . not dead . . . they're living . . . they will live again. No, I know nobody speaks Yiddish much anymore, but that doesn't mean they won't ever speak it . . . You don't want them cluttering your office. I see. I understand. I'll come down as soon as I can, in a week or so, I need to visit my parents anyway. Yes. Save them for me. Don't bury them. Please.

(Aaron hangs up the phone. It rings again.)

Aaron: Hello? Yes — you saw my sign? A whole basement full? A truck? You didn't know what to do with them. Right. Right. Let me see what I can do, give me a few days. No, no, I'll be there. Give me your number. I'll call you. Yes, I want them. Thank you. Good-bye.

(Aaron hangs up the phone. The phone rings again. Lights fade out as Aaron answers it.)

Scene 7. Dr. Wisse's office.

(Dr. Wisse is sitting at her desk. Aaron enters.)

Dr. Wisse: Aaron — how are you? I haven't heard from you in weeks.

Aaron: I haven't heard from myself! All I've been doing, since I put up those signs, has been picking up books! My apartment is full — I can't even find the refrigerator. It's no way to live! What do I do now . . . with all these books? I can't read them all at once.

Dr. Wisse: Well, I don't know. We should find a place for them.

Aaron: You have contacts with the library at McGill. Can you see if they want them?

Dr. Wisse: That's not a solution. No offense, Aaron, but most people at McGill aren't running out to find copies of S.Y. Agnon.

Aaron: So what do you suggest?

Dr. Wisse: It seems they belong in a place where people who want Yiddish books can find them easily. A place that would specialize in Yiddish books . . . a place that would help the general population learn Yiddish, learn to love Yiddish books and culture . . .

Aaron: So where do I find such a place?

Dr. Wisse: Oh, Aaron. It doesn't exist.

Aaron: Doesn't exist! Meanwhile, I can't get any sleep — people are calling me night and day! My Mother must have gotten the word out to the entire East Coast! People are insisting I come get their books . . . before they die.

Dr. Wisse: You should find some helpers. It sounds exhausting.

Aaron: And what shall I live on — while I'm saving Yiddish culture? I'm a graduate student — I have no money!

Dr. Wisse: There should be funding for such a project. It's marvelous, collecting all these treasures. I'll give you some names of some prominent Jewish philanthropists. Someone will give you funding.

Aaron: Okay. Let's say I get funding. And help. And I travel around this summer, collecting Yiddish books. What then, Dr. Wisse?

Dr. Wisse: I wish I knew, Aaron. I have faith in you. You'll think of something.

Aaron: I suppose I could . . . I suppose I could take a leave of absence from school. For a year. Or two at the most. I could find a little space somewhere . . . I'm sure some big *macher* would donate a little library where we could put these books — at least preserve them. I could get the thing started, you know? I could take a leave of absence from school . . . just for a year. That's all.

Dr. Wisse: Aaron, it seems to me that you were born at an auspicious time. Here you are 23 years old with the energy and passion to collect these books — just as a generation is reaching the end of its time here on earth. Five years ago, no one would have wanted to part with these books. Five years from now, the books might be gone. The time is right, Aaron. School will wait for you.

Aaron: School will wait. You're right, Dr. Wisse. Thank you.

Dr. Wisse: *Zi gezunt,* Aaron, and *Mazel Tov!*

(They shake hands and Aaron exits. Lights down.)

Scene 8. Mr. Spiegelman's apartment in Brooklyn.

(Aaron knocks on Mr. Spiegelman's door.) .

Aaron: Hello? Hello? Is there a Mr. Spiegelman there?

Spiegelman: *(Spiegelman peeks out of the door.)* Who wants to know?

Aaron: Uh . . . me. It's Aaron Lansky. The one you spoke with on the phone. From Canada. I drove all the way down here to Brooklyn to get your Yiddish books. I'm driving all over New York, New Jersey, Pennsylvania . . . to pick up books like yours. Could I please . . . come in . . . to get the books?

Spiegelman: How do I know it's you?

Aaron: Uh . . . well . . . I have a driver's license.

Spiegelman: Nonsense! Anyone can buy a license nowadays!

Aaron: I just want your books, Mr. Spiegelman. I'm not going to harm you.

Spiegelman: So what do you want with the books?

Aaron: I want to save them. It's a crime. Books were burned in Nazi Germany. Here in America, they're just thrown away.

Spiegelman: If you're the Yiddish *boychick*, you gotta prove it. Sing me something.

Aaron: In Yiddish?

Spiegelman: No, in Chinese! Of course in Yiddish.

Aaron: All right . . . But I'm not really a good singer —

Spiegelman: Sing!

(The Muse enters and starts singing "Rozhinkes Mit Mandlen."[10] *Aaron follows along.)*

Muse: *Unter Yidele's vigele*
Sheyt a klor-vays tsigele
Dos tsigele iz geforn handlen
Dos vet zayn dayn baruf
Rozhinkes mit mandlen
Shlof zhe, Yidele, shlof.[11]

Spiegelman: Not bad. Come in. (*He opens the door all the way and Aaron enters.*)

Aaron: Uummm, thank you. Where are the books?

Spiegelman: The books you want? Not so fast. Sit down. Drink a *glessela tey.*[12]

---

10 "Raisins and Almonds," a famous Yiddish lullaby
11 Under the little Jewish boy's crib
   There's a bright, white little goat
   The goat has gone to market
   This will be your calling [career]
   Raisins with almonds
   Sleep, little Jewish boy, sleep.
12 A glass of tea.

Aaron: Thank you.

Spiegelman: These books, they're not just any books, you know. My Mother, she would go for a week without breakfast and lunch, just to buy a book. She loved literature. My Mother would read to us, in the morning when we woke . . . she'd read us fairy tales and lullabies . . . she'd read us poetry . . . from these very books.

Aaron: I can imagine . . . how important these books are to you.

Spiegelman: Can you? Can you imagine? These books — the ones I have here I brought with me when I left Europe. I was 16, stubborn, wild. I wanted to live in America. (*Pause.*) When the war first started, I tried to get them to come over — my Mother, my Father, my sisters and their families. They said things would get better. They wouldn't come.

Aaron: I'm so sorry. You don't have children . . . or grandchildren . . . to pass the books on to?

Spiegelman: My son lives in California . . . he's a big shot in the movie business. He doesn't want them, can't be bothered. My daughter says, "Pop, I can't read them! You never taught me Yiddish." It's true. I only wanted my children should be American. I didn't realize what would be lost.

Aaron: I'm honored that you're giving the books to me, Mr. Spiegelman. I'll take good care of them.

Spiegelman: You're building a library, is that it?

Aaron: Um, yes, sort of.

Spiegelman: Sort of what? Is it a library or isn't it?

Aaron: Yes . . . I want to build a Yiddish cultural center . . . I'm trying to work on getting the funds we need.

Spiegelman: Funds? That's all you need. Funds? (*He takes a few crinkled dollar bills from his pocket*). You'll get the money. Here's a start, *boychick*. Here you go.

Aaron: Oh, Mr. Spiegelman, I can't take your money.

Spiegelman: We'll get you more, don't worry. Now, you better get upstairs. Everybody's waiting.

Aaron: Everybody? Everybody who?

Spiegelman: Everyone in the building, of course. I told them you're coming. They all have books for you.

Aaron: You told your entire building?

Spiegelman: My girlfriend Betty lives on the eighth floor and she told everyone up there. My girlfriend Pearl lives on ten and she told everyone from ten up . . .

Aaron: You have two girlfriends?

Spiegelman: One can't see and the other can't hear, so between us all, we do okay. Come on *boychick*, I'll introduce you.

Aaron: I hope my truck can handle it . . . it's a second, well third hand *tranta*.[13]

Spiegelman: A regular *pakn treger*. That's what you are kid. A *pakn treger*.

---

13 Broken down thing

(They exit together. The Muse watches and sings "Rozhinkes Mit Mandlen.")

Scene 9. The Philanthropist's office.

Philanthropist: Good morning. You must be Aaron Lansky.

Aaron: Yes, good morning, sir. Nice to meet you. Thank you for taking time out of your busy schedule to talk with me.

Philanthropist: Dr. Ruth Wisse suggested we speak. I certainly try and listen to such a distinguished professor. (*Pause.*) What can I help you with, Aaron?

Aaron: I am a Ph.D. student in Dr. Wisse's department at McGill University, focusing on Eastern European Jewish Studies. As part of my studies, I have been reading Yiddish books . . . the classics, Sholem Aleichem, Sholem Asch . . .

Philanthropist: Go on.

Aaron: It was hard for me to locate these books in Yiddish through our library system at McGill. I started looking in the greater Jewish community in Montreal. Soon, I started receiving hundreds of calls — older people, mostly, who wanted to donate their Yiddish books to someone . . . but they didn't know who would want them.

Philanthropist: And you, Mr. Lansky, want them?

Aaron: So far, I've collected thousands of books . . .

without really trying. If I had the money to hire a staff and collect these books and organize them and . . .

Philanthropist: So you're here to ask for money.

Aaron: Well, yes.

Philanthropist: To save Yiddish books?

Aaron: That's right.

Philanthropist: Mr. Lansky, the Jewish community has many needs. We must support Israel. We must fight against intermarriage. We must get the unaffiliated to join synagogue communities. And you come in here . . . asking me for money for Yiddish books? Yiddish is yesterday. I am helping the Jewish community of today . . . become the Jewish community of tomorrow. The only ones who care about Yiddish books are academics like you who want them for research.

Aaron: I'm not an academic! I mean I am . . . but I'm more . . . I carry these books by the boxful from old people's homes back to my apartment where I can't even sit down anymore! I care about the Jewish community of today and tomorrow, too. They know hardly anything of this literature. I want to bring it to them. We can't know who we are today without understanding where we come from.

Philanthropist: You're young, Mr. Lansky. Soon you'll grow up and put this pipe dream aside. You need to earn a living. There's no money in becoming a *pakn treger*.

Aaron: I believe there will be the money I need. Even if it comes from the change purses of old men and women, even if it means sacrifices on my part. I have to save these books!

Philanthropist: Best of luck, Mr. Lansky. And do keep me posted . . . about the opening of your library.

Aaron: Thanks . . . for your time. (*Under his breath.*) *A shainem dank in pupik* — thanks for nothing.

(*Aaron exits.*)

Philanthropist: Yiddish books? What do they want next — a revival of Klezmer music? (*Starts laughing.*) Yiddish and Klezmer . . . I can see it now!

(*Lights down.*)

Scene 10. Aaron's parents' home.

Father: Just explain it to me, once more.

Aaron: There are Yiddish books — all over the world — that are being thrown out because no one wants them . . .

Mother: And it's your job to drop out of school to save these books?

Aaron: Not drop out, take a leave of absence.

Father: And you want to start this Yiddish library?

Aaron: Cultural center. Book exchange.

Mother: With what funds? You've been turned down by every major Jewish philanthropist.

Aaron: I don't need much money — just enough to rent a room somewhere. Buy some stationary. A phone might be nice.

Father: And you will find this money from . . .

Aaron: You wouldn't believe it. I've collected money already. Everywhere I go, these old men and women give me dollar bills . . . they want me to do this, they believe in me. I've collected money at least to start out.

Mother: But Aaron, what will you live on?

Aaron: If I can work the rest of the summer, I can put away some money to live on in the fall while I'm getting this started.

Father: You have a job?

Aaron: Yeah. If I can leave the books here for a few months, I'm going up to Maine, to pick blueberries.

Mother: A college education, in a doctoral program . . . and you're going to pick grapes?

Aaron: Blueberries.

Father: Aaron, you're an adult. You need to make decisions on your own and live with the consequences. If this is what you want to do . . .

Mother: Then go — with our blessing.

Aaron: Thanks, Mom, Dad. I've got to go pack some things.

Mother: Aaron . . . you will come back — for these books, I mean?

Aaron: I'm committed to them, Mom. Like I've never been to anything else!

(Aaron exits. Mother and Father sigh. Lights down.)

Scene 11. Three months later.

(Aaron is sorting books at the first "book center.")

Aaron: Let's see here . . . three copies, in decent condition, of *The Brothers Ashkenaz* —

(A Reporter from The Boston Globe *knocks and enters.)*

Reporter: Hello, can you help me? I'm terribly lost. I'm looking for a place called "The Yiddish Book Exchange." I'm to meet with Aaron Lansky. I'd call him, but he doesn't have a telephone —

Aaron: Hi, I'm Aaron! You're the reporter from the *Globe*?

Reporter: Are you pulling my leg? I drove all the way from Boston to Amherst . . . for this? A kid sitting at a picnic table with a government surplus typewriter?

Aaron: I know it doesn't look like much . . . but there's more here than meets the eye. I think you could have a great story here.

Reporter: About what? All the nuts who send out press releases?

Aaron: This is legitimate . . . I promise you. Look around . . . I know it doesn't look like much . . . but in just a few months, I've saved thousands of Yiddish books. Out of print books, many carried over from Europe. I'm trying to catalogue them . . . so people can use them. I've found these just by word of mouth. If I could get some publicity, I'm sure I could find thousands more books like these.

Reporter: I need a human interest for this story. Who are you, why are you doing this, and why should anyone care?

Aaron: Please, sit down. Drink some tea. You want stories? I'll tell you.

(The Muse walks through the book stacks, browsing.)

Muse: Novels? Oy, I love novels! Aaronalah, *Zunikeh* — dear one, don't you worry. I'll put a little pickle juice in this one's tea. A story he'll write, like you never saw! *The Boston Globe*, no less! I see it — the future — books everywhere — beautiful Yiddish books . . . coming home.

Reporter: You're right, Mr. Lansky. I think there is . . . quite a story here.

(Reporter shakes Aaron's hand and exits.)

Scene 12. Two weeks later.

(Aaron is running around the Book Exchange. The helpers are busy working, too. The phone is ringing constantly.)

Aaron: All right . . . Tom and Ellen, you take the truck today and head to Connecticut. There are five stops total you need to make. Sam, you'll help me stack the books that were dropped off last night. Sheila, you can start cataloguing them. Write all the titles and authors on these cards. *Oy*, the phone again —

(He picks up the phone.)

Aaron: Yiddish Book Exchange. Yes? You read the article in *The Boston Globe*? Yes, that's us . . . What? Excuse me? Eight thousand books? Where? Oh my — you've just saved them . . . no, no, we'll be there!

(He hangs up the phone, looks astonished.)

Aaron: What I just said . . . cancel everything. The timing . . . I can't believe it. Someone read the article in the *Globe* yesterday. A friend mailed it to him from Boston. This guy lives in Brooklyn . . . and he walked by these dumpsters . . . he thinks there are probably eight thousand Yiddish books . . . (*Pause.*) We'll save them. We'll make trips. We'll find trucks. I have the address . . . let's go!

(Everyone starts to exit. Aaron pauses, and looks around at the room.)

Aaron: The old Yiddish saying, "man plans and God laughs" — I understand it now. I don't know where my life is going . . . I don't know what will happen with this crazy endeavor . . . but I do know one thing . . . it's out of my hands.

(He exits. The Muse enters and sings. "Rozhinkes Mit Mandlen.")

Muse: *Unter Yidele's vigele*
Sheyt a klor-vays tsigele
Dos tsigele iz geforn handlen

Dos vet zayn dayn baruf
Rozhinkes mit mandlen
Shlof zhe, Yidele, shlof.

(At the end of her song, everyone in the cast enters and fills the stage. People may be dressed in fancy clothes, etc.)

Muse: Ladies and gentlemen. I am honored to welcome you here today . . . to the inauguration of the brand new National Yiddish Book Center. Over 18 years ago, a young man named Aaron Lansky sacrificed his time, his sweat, his own academic career . . . to find a home for our great Yiddish stories. Aaron started with nothing — only the hopes and dreams of the individuals that he met. As the years went on, others joined in his vision. Individual donations helped to build this wonderful place — an eight million dollar undertaking that now houses over 25,000 Yiddish books. Because of Aaron's work, many major university libraries now have Yiddish book collections. And people can come here, to the Center, to take classes in Yiddish, to visit the exhibition rooms, to participate in summer programs for college students, visit our lending library. What you have here today is something we couldn't have dreamed of 20 years ago — Yiddish culture is reborn! We thank you, Aaron Lansky, for your labor of love.

(Everyone applauds.)

Aaron: Sometimes people ask me, how is it that Yiddish language and culture isn't doomed? After the Holocaust . . . after assimilation in America . . . how is it that Yiddish doesn't go away? When people ask me this, I remember the words of one of our greatest Yiddish scholars, Max Weinrich: "Yiddish has magic. It will outwit history."

(Aaron and the Muse embrace.)

Aaron: Thank you, my Muse.

(Lights down.)

Aaron Lansky continues to serve as President of the National Yiddish Book Center, housed in a beautiful new facility on ten acres purchased from Hampshire College in Amherst, Massachusetts. Aaron was the deserving recipient of a MacArthur Fellowship for his outstanding work. The institution he founded houses the largest collection of Yiddish books in history, and serves as a major cultural and educational center for the promotion of Yiddish. More than 1.4 million volumes have been rescued by the Center, as well as 160,000 mint condition pieces of Yiddish and Hebrew sheet music. Over 1,000 books continue to arrive by mail and UPS every week. Through the Center, Yiddish collections at 437 major libraries in 20 countries have been established or strengthened. The Center has a full-time staff of 30 and 10 fellows and Work-Study Students. For more information on the National Yiddish Book center, check out their web site at www.yiddishbookcenter.org, or call 413-256-4900. If you are in the Amherst area, stop by and thank Aaron Lansky for being a Jewish hero.

Yitzhak Rabin: Soldier Turned Peacemaker

Characters*

Reporter
Miri Aloni
Yitzhak Rabin
Young Yitzhak
Nehemiah Rabin (Father)
Rosa Cohen (Mother)
Rachel Rabin
Teacher
Leah Schlossberg Rabin
Soldier
Recruits
Moshe Dayan
President Nixon
Assistant
Shimon Peres
Israeli citizens

*Actors can play multiple characters if necessary.

Costumes

Rabin should wear military clothes or a suit as appropriate. Reporter, Leah, Shimon Peres, and Israeli citizens should wear contemporary clothing for the opening and end of the play. For the earlier scenes, you might research clothing during the 1920s to the 1960s in Israel.

Setting

The opening and closing scenes should have the feeling of being set outside, in Tel Aviv's central square. You might construct a platform or podium for Rabin, Leah, Shimon Peres, and Miri Aloni to stand on. The other scenes need little or no set pieces.

Sound Effects

A tape of gunshots and an ambulance siren will help to create the needed effect. You could also use more "symbolic" effects, such as a cymbal crash to act as the gunfire. It is important for any performance that you let the audience know if you are using taped gunshots (a program note works well). Use a recording of the "The Song of Peace." This can be located from any Israeli music source.

(Yitzhak and Leah Rabin, Shimon Peres, and Miri Aloni are standing in front of a large crowd of Israeli citizens at a peace demonstration in Tel Aviv. Reporter stands off to the side and comments.)

Reporter: *Rabbotai u'Geverotai, Shalom*! Ladies and gentlemen, we are broadcasting live from the Kings of Israel Square in Tel Aviv. As you can see, thousands are here in support of the newly signed peace treaty between Israel and the Palestinians. We have also been treated to entertainment by some of Israel's best known performers. They are here to show their support for our Prime Minister, Yitzhak Rabin, who orchestrated the peace accords. The energy here is amazing — people are singing, dancing, celebrating! Of course, protestors from the right wing are also here. They have opposed making concessions to the Palestinians of land for peace. We will cover their protest rally after the peace program concludes. I've just received word that Prime Minister Rabin, who is here tonight with his wife Leah, is about to deliver his much anticipated speech.

(The Reporter steps to the side and Rabin steps forward for his speech.)

Rabin: I want to thank each one of you for coming here to take a stand against violence and for peace. I was a soldier for 27 years. I fought our enemies when there was no prospect for peace. But now there is a great chance for peace. We must seize it.

(The audience erupts with applause and cheers.)

Rabin: This will not be painless for Israel. But peace is preferable to war. This rally must send a message to the Israeli public, to the Jews of the world, to the multitudes in the Arab lands, and to the world at large . . . that Israel wants peace, supports peace. And for this, I thank you for being here tonight.

(Audience again applauds and cheers.)

Reporter: As you can see, the crowd here in the Kings of Israel Square is very excited. The Prime Minister's words were inspiring and affirmed that peace is surely on the way. Now singer Miri Aloni is coming to the podium. Aloni will lead the crowd in the singing of "The Song of Peace." Well, it appears that Mr. Rabin, his wife Leah, and Foreign Minister Shimon Peres are staying on stage for the song. Let's watch.

Alon: The "Song of Peace" is a rallying cry for what we believe must happen now — peace in the land of Israel. Please join us, as we sing together.

(Recording of "The Song of Peace" plays in the background. All on stage join in the song.)

Reporter: What a night! Surely this rally will be remembered and cherished in Israel's history. The crowd is slowly dispersing. Prime Minister Rabin and his wife have just exited the stage. As promised, we will now interview some of the right-wing protestors who . . .

(The sound of gunshots and screaming is heard. Mass confusion. Ambulance sirens blare.)

Reporter: What's that? Something has happened? I am reporting live from central Tel Aviv. We have just heard gunshots. Someone has been shot! Stay tuned . . . we will be bringing you the latest coverage. *Rehga*, I've just received a note. Oh, no, Prime Minister Rabin has been shot!

(For a moment, there is total silence on the stage.)

Reporter: People of Israel, pray for this brave leader . . . whose life may be in grave danger. Let us pray for him and reflect on all that he has given to the people of Israel.

(The Reporter and the crowd slowly disperse. In the next scenes, the life of Yitzhak Rabin, from his childhood to the present, is dramatized. In between, the Reporter reappears to give updates on Rabin's condition.)

(In Rabin's childhood home. Father, Mother, Young Yitzhak, and Rachel are present.)

Mother: Yitzhak! Rachel! It's time for school.

Young Yitzhak: I'm almost ready, *Ima* . . . and so is Rachel.

Mother: I need to leave. We have a meeting of the "Haganah" leadership before work. This is a critical time.

With the Arab attacks starting on some of our Jewish settlements, I will need to give more time to our defense organization.

Young Yitzhak: Does that mean you'll be away from home more, Mother?

Father: Yitzhak, I will be home this evening to make dinner for you and Rachel. Your Mother is helping all of us . . . making it safer for us to have Jewish settlements here in Palestine.

Mother: Good-bye, Yitzhak. Good-bye, Rachel. Be good today. Rachel, listen to your older brother. He's in charge of you. Good-bye, Nehemiah. I hope I won't be too late.

(She leaves.)

Young Yitzhak: *Abba*, is it like this in other countries? Do fathers and mothers have to stay out late to make plans for their country?

Father: Not exactly. We live in an exciting time, Yitzhak. Jewish people from all over Europe, like your *Ima* and me, are coming home to the land of Palestine. We believe in Zionism — a return to our biblical homeland. This is where we can create a modern, Jewish culture. It just takes a lot of work and sacrifice. That's why *Ima* and I have to go to work and to meetings . . . and sometimes, when attacked, we have to fight.

Rachel: I don't want you or *Ima* to fight, *Abba*. I don't want you to get hurt.

Father: Don't worry, Rachel, we will be fine. Besides, you also have Yitzhak to take care of you. You're in good hands. Now, I have to get to work, children. *Ima* and I love you very much.

(He kisses them and leaves.)

Young Yitzhak: Come on, Rachel. It's time for school.

Rachel: I don't want to go today. I want to stay home and play!

Young Yitzhak: Rachel, didn't you listen to *Abba*? It's going to take lots of work to make a Jewish homeland. We haven't had one in almost two thousand years. We have to go to school so we can learn a lot of things . . . so we can help the Jewish people. You want to help, don't you?

Rachel: Yes . . . but I'd rather play.

Young Yitzhak: Come on!

(They exit. The Reporter comes to the side of the stage.)

Reporter: We are still waiting for reports of Prime Minister Rabin's condition. There is no official word just yet. Rabin has been one of Israel's greatest citizens, serving our country since before the War of Independence.

(Yitzhak at age 16 and one of his teachers appears.)

Teacher: Yitzhak, I have good news for you. You are going to receive a prize this year for being our top agricultural student. Congratulations.

Yitzhak: Really? Wow — I can't believe it. I didn't think my final project was that good.

Teacher: Your work all semester has been top notch. You really understand agriculture, both the scientific theory and the practical application. You're just a born farmer!

Yitzhak: I always dreamed of some day owning a farm here in Palestine, and working on this land where our ancestors walked. I imagined orange groves and date trees and maybe chicken and sheep . . .

Teacher: We need farmers like you, Yitzhak, farmers dedicated to the land. It's not easy work to farm in the desert, but it can be done. It must be done.

Yitzhak: Someday, maybe, I'll become a farmer, but not now. I have other plans after graduation.

Teacher: I had a feeling you might.

Yitzhak: I will be a full-time soldier. I must. There is too great a need for soldiers who can fight. First we must secure the land . . . make sure we have a place to farm, to build our country. We can't stay under British control much longer. We need our independence.

Teacher: I have heard great reports about your military training, too, Yitzhak. The Haganah will want you to join . . . if you are willing to sacrifice.

Yitzhak: I appreciate everything I've learned here at school. But with a war breaking out in Europe as well as our struggle here, there is no choice for me but to fight . . .

Teacher: I understand. All of us must sacrifice in some way if this land is to be ours. *(Pause.)* You will still receive the Agriculture award, Yitzhak. For that, you should be proud.

(They shake hands and exit.)

Reporter: During World War II, Rabin was invited by Moshe Dayan to join a special force called the Palmach. At 19, Rabin was the youngest on the force, but certainly one of the fiercest fighters.

(Rabin and Dayan enter.)

Dayan: Yitzhak Rabin. I've heard about you. How long have you been in the Haganah?

Rabin: For two years, sir.

Dayan: As you know, Rabin, World War Two is accelerating. We have to help the British maintain their hold here. Enemies from the Third Reich will try to penetrate Palestine next.

Rabin: I understand, Sir. I am ready to do whatever must be done.

Dayan: Are you are willing to go on special missions . . . cross enemy lines . . . ?

Rabin: Whatever it takes, I will do.

Dayan: There is a mission that calls for sneaking across the Syrian border. Are you prepared to leave your home?

Rabin: Tell me where and when, Sir.

Dayan: You are a good man, a leader, Rabin. This is your test. Don't disappoint me.

(Rabin salutes him. They exit.)

Reporter: We are standing by live, waiting to hear about the condition of Yitzhak Rabin. The nation . . . the world . . . is waiting . . . praying for the soldier who became a peacemaker. As you may recall, Yitzhak Rabin played a critical role in defending Palestine during World War Two and in fighting for our independence, in 1948. During the War of Independence, Rabin commanded the Har-El Brigade, which kept open crucial passageways between Jerusalem and the Sea. That year was also important to Rabin for other reasons. That was the year he and Leah were married.

(Rabin and Soldier enter.)

Soldier: The new recruits are here. They're ready to start basic training.

Rabin: Let's see what we have this time. We'll have to whip them into shape quickly. The fighting is escalating. Bring them in.

Soldier: Come on, come on . . . move . . . move, move. Attention!

(The new soldiers enter and stand in line. Leah Schlossberg is among them. Rabin looks them over.)

Rabin: *(Clearing his throat, so as to get the attention of a soldier.)* Aaahhhmmm.

Soldier: Are you okay, Sir?

Rabin: I need to speak with you. Privately.

Soldier: Yes, Sir. At ease, recruits. *(To Rabin.)* What is it, Sir?

Rabin: That recruit — second in line. I've seen her before.

Soldier: Uh . . . yes? Is there something wrong, Sir?

Rabin: Wrong? With her? Absolutely not, she's beautiful. Look at her . . . I mean . . .

Soldier: Perhaps we should give the recruits a short break before starting training, Sir. Perhaps you'd like to get . . . a cold drink?

Rabin: Cold drink . . . break . . .very good, yes. What . . . what did you say her name is?

Soldier: Let's see, it's right here. Leah Schlossberg, from Tel Aviv.

Rabin: That's where I've seen her! Thank you, Soldier.

Soldier: Commander Rabin will grant you a short break before we begin basic training. I suggest you take advantage of it.

(The recruits start to exit. Rabin approaches Leah.)

Rabin: Excuse me, wait, wait, Leah . . . I mean Private Schlossberg.

Leah: Yes, Sir. What is it?

Rabin: I think I know you . . . from Tel Aviv, isn't it?

Leah: We've never formally met, Sir, but you've been following me around for years, watching me.

Rabin: You saw me?

Leah: Come on, please! Thank goodness you're a better soldier than you are an admirer. If not, we'd surely be losing the war.

Rabin: I used to see you, walking home from school . . . or going out with your girlfriends. I couldn't believe how beautiful you were . . . I mean, are . . . I mean . . .

Leah: So, why didn't you ever come talk to me?

Rabin: I'm actually very shy. I always have been. Since I was a boy. I'm good at listening, watching, but I've never been good at expressing my feelings.

Leah: A famous military man like you? You're not afraid to face the enemies, but you're afraid to face . . . a girl?

Rabin: I'm facing you now, Leah. I'm not afraid.

Leah: You're my commander. I have to listen to you now!

Rabin: We can have you transferred to a different unit. I would like to take you out . . . for coffee, maybe, or dinner . . . soon . . . when there's a cease fire.

Leah: If we wait that long, we may be old and gray before we go out!

Rabin: You're right . . . tonight! I'll meet you at 1900 hours.

Leah: Yes, Sir!

Rabin: Uh . . . you're . . . you can take your break now.

Leah: Don't stand me up, Sir. I hate it when a man arrives late.

(She exits. He watches her and then follows.)

Reporter: After the War of Independence, Yitzhak and Leah began their family. Daughter Dalia and son Yuval were born in an independent Israel, which their parents and grandparents had helped to form. Yitzhak gave up his dream of becoming a farmer. It was clear, in the 1950s, that he was needed in Israel's military forces. He received promotion after promotion until, in 1963, he was appointed Chief of Staff. For the next three years he trained, planned, and built the army that would, in 1967, go on to victory in the Six-Day War. As a result of that war, Jerusalem was united under Jewish control for the first time in over 2,000 years. With that success, Rabin moved from the military to the political scene. In 1968, he became Israel's ambassador to the United States. He and his family went to America.

(President Nixon enters, followed by Rabin.)

Nixon: I see you've developed quite a friendship with Henry Kissinger.

Rabin: Yes, Kissinger has been very understanding and sympathetic to our cause. Because of the cold war, Israel is especially important as an outpost for democracy in the Middle East. The 23 Arab countries surrounding us are supported with Soviet money and armaments.

Nixon: You Israelis are tough. You are the underdog, and I tend to favor the underdog.

Rabin: President Nixon, it is critical that you not only like Israel, but that you understand how much we need U.S. arms and support. These must be ready for us whenever there is a crisis.

Nixon: What crisis? You won the Six-Day War. Jerusalem is united under your control.

Rabin: The situation is still tense, tenuous. I would rather come here to talk about peace and not have to worry about getting U.S. planes, but I cannot. Our country is young and vulnerable, and our enemies are always ready to attack.

Nixon: You don't need to worry, Yitzhak. You are a western country. We will support you. *(Pause.)* So, how do you like it here in America?

Rabin: I love America. I love your spirit, your culture, your sports, and the Jewish community here. I used to hear about America from my Father. He came here when he was a boy, from Russia. He lived in Chicago for ten years. I always thought Chicago was a little village, the way he talked about it. He loved it here, but he had to leave. He wanted to build a homeland for the Jewish people, a place where refugees from all over Europe could build a Jewish nation, with democratic principles. That's where I belong, too, Mr. President.

Nixon: Come, let me show you the rest of the White House. Then we'll meet up with Leah and Pat. You'll be our guest for lunch.

(They walk off together.)

Reporter: Yitzhak Rabin was Ambassador to the United States until 1974. He returned to Israel and served various positions in the Israeli government. In 1992, he regained leadership of the Labor Party and was appointed Prime Minister. At the same time, Israeli troops withdrew from Lebanon. This turned out to be an opportunity to begin peace talks.

(Rabin and Assistant enter.)

Assistant: Mr. Rabin, President Clinton is on the phone.

Rabin: Thank you. Hello? Yes? Bill? Fine, fine. Yes . . . I agree. We want to . . . no, no, we'll have to negotiate that. I understand. Of course. Of course. Tell him that. Thank you.

Assistant: What is it?

Rabin: Clinton will help us. Arafat wants to sit down and talk.

Assistant: Yasir Arafat, Chairman of the Palestine Liberation Organization?

Rabin: The one. Even a year or two ago . . . this would have been unthinkable. Maybe we are all growing tired of the bloodshed . . . of seeing families destroyed, our sons killed, our children wounded. And why? We fight over land and living space for two peoples. *(Pause.)* All my life I have fought to build a Jewish state. We have our homeland. When will we stop fighting? I am willing to sit down with Arafat. Shimon Peres and I will go. It's worth a try.

Assistant: But what about the right-wing? There are people who think we shouldn't negotiate, no matter what.

Rabin: I hope they will come to see . . . that I would never, ever risk Israel's security. I believe instead that I am working to make a safer place for our children and our grandchildren. We can't go on with this bloodshed.

Assistant: What about the press? What kind of statement should we issue?

Rabin: We should simply tell the truth, that President Clinton is facilitating talks between us and Arafat. That's all. When there's more news, we'll announce it.

(They exit.)

Reporter: In 1993, Rabin made major news. He signed the Declaration of Principles with PLO Chairman Yasir Arafat. The Declaration included mutual recognition between Israel and the Palestinians. It even included Palestinian self-rule in Gaza and Jericho. Because of this, Rabin, Arafat, and Israeli Foreign Minister Shimon Peres were awarded the Nobel Prize for Peace.

(Rabin and Leah enter.)

Leah: Yitzhak, I can't believe the news! The Nobel Prize — this is fantastic!

Yitzhak: Well, it also goes to Peres, who worked so hard . . . and of course to Arafat.

Leah: I know. I am proud of all of you. For the first time since 1948, we have the hope for real peace. And the world has acknowledged that.

Yitzhak: I think that most Israelis are proud and happy, too. Yet there are some who aren't so pleased. They are becoming very vocal. They will never accept Palestinian self-rule. They feel I've made too many concessions. *(Pause.)* I hate to say this, but I fear both the extremist hawks and the extremist doves. They scare me.

Leah: Having received the Nobel Peace Prize, the people who oppose you will have to think again. They'll appreciate your work . . . in time. That's politics, Yitzhak. You know that. Can you believe that it's already 1994? We've been married forty-six years!

Yitzhak: I hope I have been a good husband and a good father. I know you didn't bargain for such a public life.

Leah: We've had a grand life. You are a wonderful husband . . . and father . . . and grandfather. In fact, the family has planned a celebration in honor of our prize winner. I wasn't supposed to tell you, but we should go, we'll be late.

Yitzhak: Leah . . .

Leah: We're late, really, come on . . .

Yitzhak: I love you, Leah. That's all I wanted to say.

Leah: And I, Yitzhak, love you.

(They embrace and exit.)

Reporter: The Peace process continued. Acceptance of the Oslo II accords was tenuous. Though the majority of citizens supported Prime Minister Rabin's steps toward peace, others felt strongly that he was giving the Palestinians too much autonomy and getting nothing in return. In the fall of 1995, Rabin's supporters planned a pro-peace, anti-violence rally in Tel Aviv. Thousands of Israelis were in the Kings of Israel Square when Rabin took the stage.

(What follows is a "reenactment" of the opening scene.)

Rabin: I want to thank each one of you for coming here to take a stand against violence and for peace. I was a soldier for 27 years. I fought our enemies when there was no prospect for peace. But now there is a great chance for peace. We must seize it.

(The audience erupts with applause and cheers.)

Rabin: This will not be painless for Israel. But peace is preferable to war. This rally must send a message to the Israeli public, to the Jews of the world, to the multitudes in the Arab lands, and to the world at large . . . that Israel wants peace, supports peace. And for this, I thank you for being here tonight.

(Audience again applauds and cheers.)

Reporter: As you can see, the crowd here in the Kings of Israel Square is very excited. The Prime Minister's words were inspiring and affirmed that peace is surely on the way. Now singer Miri Aloni is coming to the podium. She will lead the crowd in the singing of "The Song of Peace." Well, it appears that Mr. Rabin, his wife Leah, and Foreign Minister Shimon Peres are staying on stage for the song. Let's watch.

Aloni: The "The Song of Peace" is a rallying cry for what we believe must happen now — peace in the land of Israel. Please join us, as we sing together.

(Recording of "The Song of Peace" plays in the background. All on stage join in the song. Rabin and Leah exit.)

Reporter: This . . . just in. Prime Minister Yitzhak Rabin has been shot . . . and fatally wounded. Our leader was shot to death by one of our own, a Jewish assassin, suspected of being a right wing fanatic. Rabin was 73 years old. He was born in Palestine and grew up with our young country. Yitzhak Rabin, we will never forget you. Our fearless soldier turned fearless peacemaker. We will make your memory live on in our actions and our hopes. May your memory be for a blessing.

(The ensemble of actors slowly walks across the stage as if passing before Rabin's coffin. They quietly hum "Hatikvah.")

Reporter: Your legacy of peace and hope will live on.

Yitzhak Rabin graduated from the Kadourie Agricultural School in Kfar Tabor, and in 1941, joined the Palmach, the commando unit of the Jewish Defense Forces. During the War of Independence, he directed the defense of Jerusalem and also fought the Egyptians in the Negev. He played a major role in designing the strategies that enabled Israel to win the Six-Day War. After his retirement from the army, Rabin became the Israeli ambassador to the United States. When he returned home, he entered politics and was elected to the Knesset as a member of the Labour Party. He was Golda Meir's Minister of Labor, then became Prime Minister of Israel in 1974, serving until 1977. Following this, he served as Defense Minister for six years. In 1992, he was elected Prime Minister for a second time, and served until his assassination on November 4, 1995. He was shot by Yigal Amir, a 25-year-old member of a Jewish extremist group. Amir has said he shot Rabin to halt the peace process with the Palestinians. Rabin's work and life have not been forgotten. Working for peace against all odds is Rabin's greatest legacy.

Hannah Senesh: Tefilat HaAdam

Characters:

Hannah
Ensemble:
 Bela
 Rabbi
 Danny
 Ari
 Guard
 Catherine
 Eva
 Grandma
 8ᵗʰ Form Girl
 Irma
 Miriam
 George
 Headmaster
 Gaby
Sea Captain

Costumes

All Ensemble players should be dressed in simple black clothing. Hannah may wear black with colorful scarves, etc.

Props

A parachute is most effective for the dramatic staging of this play. If a parachute is unavailable, a simple sheet will suffice.

Staging

This one-act play is divided into three sections. Each section opens with Hannah and the Ensemble holding onto the outer edges of a parachute. They sing *"Eli, Eli "* as they circle. When the song finishes, they drop the parachute and the action begins. The Ensemble remains onstage throughout the play. The style of the play is deliberately theatrical, not naturalistic. "Props" tables can line one or both sides of the stage, holding all of the costume and prop pieces characters will need. Characters simply pick up and put down props as the play goes on. When characters are not speaking, they may softly freeze. Creative direction can frame the various stage pictures.

Scene 1

(Hannah and the Ensemble hold the outer edges of a parachute and walk in slow, rythmic circles. They sing "Eli, Eli.")

Eli, Eli
Shelo yigamer le'olam
Hachol vehayam
Rishrush shel hamayim
Berak hashamayim
Tefilat ha'adam

My God, my God
I pray that these things never end:
The sand and the sea, the rush of the waters,
The crash of the heavens, the prayer of the heart.

(They lay the parachute down slowly, then walk upstage crisply and pose as if in a family photo.)

Bela: I am a man blessed with good fortune! It's 1927, and I'm the most successful Jewish playwright in all of

Budapest. No, make that in all of Hungary! Not only do I write a column for the most prominent newspaper in Budapest, but also my plays are performed by popular demand at the Comedy Theater! They even let me — the playwright — have some say about whom to cast! Some of these Hungarian actors — if only their talents were as big as their egos! But as for me — as I say — I am truly a fortunate man!

(Catherine coughs loudly, clearing her throat.)

Bela: Oh yes . . . even more important than my writing career is my precious family. My wife Catherine, her dear Mama, my seven-year-old son George, and, of course, six-year-old Hannah.

Hannah: Papa, I am going to be a great writer just like you!

George: I'm tired of getting our portrait done. Mama, can we go to the zoo?

Hannah: I want to go to the park!

Catherine: Bela, you make the decision for your children.

Bela: My children? But they are in the best of hands with you.

Grandma: It's settled then. On a lovely Sunday afternoon, like today, we shall visit the park *and* the zoo!

George and Hannah: Yeeeeaaaahhhh!

(All characters except Bela turn upstage and freeze.)

Bela: This was the last of such lovely outings with my family. Later that spring, I suffered a heart attack. I never awoke from my sleep.

(Bela turns upstage and puts on a prayer shawl and yarmulke. *The family stands around, as if at a grave.)*

Rabbi: George, you are your father's only son. But you are too young to recite the *Kaddish*.

George: It doesn't matter. My father was a humanist. He did not believe in prayer.

Grandma: It doesn't matter what he believed. We are Jews. *Kaddish* must be said.

Hannah: I will say it!

Catherine: Hannah, quiet darling. You aren't old enough, and – besides — you can't say it. You're a girl. Only men can recite such prayers.

Hannah: But I want to remember my Papa!

Catherine: You will remember him, darling. Papa will always be in your heart.

Hannah: My love for Papa will be like a prayer. Like a prayer that is always in my heart.

Rabbi: *Yiskadal, v'yiskadash shemay rabboh . . .*

(The words of the Rabbi become quieter. The characters freeze. Hannah, carrying schoolbooks in her arms, steps downstage.)

Hannah: The years following Papa's death were sad ones for all of us. But my brother George, my best friend, was a great comfort to me. And so were my books! I finished my four years of elementary school with high marks. My teachers noted that I excelled in writing both compositions and poetry. Maybe I would become a writer, just like Papa, after all.

Catherine: Hannah, come here. I need to talk with you about something important. A new school has just opened in Budapest, a Protestant school for girls. It is supposed to be the best school yet — with the very finest teachers and the most distinguished student body. I think your father would have wanted you to attend.

Hannah: But it's a Protestant school, Mama.

Catherine: Yes, but they will allow Catholic girls and Jewish girls to attend. You will receive special attention for your writing there.

Hannah: Oh, Mama, I want to start today! I must tell George! But first I should finish my poem. They'll want to see it. Mama, I'm working on a new poem. I think it is my best one yet.

(Hannah turns and freezes.)

Catherine: What Hannah didn't know was that the regular tuition at the school was doubled for Catholics, and Jewish girls had to pay three times the Protestant price. After Hannah's first year, when her marks came back as outstanding and she was singled out for her academic achievement, I went to the Headmaster.

(Headmaster wears glasses and carries a pipe.)

Headmaster: Yes, I see your point, Mrs. Senesh, but I'm afraid I can't change the rules for you. It's not a matter of prejudice, we're happy to have Jewish students here . . . . After all, Jews are Hungarians just like anyone else, but you must remember, this is a Protestant school. It was created by and for Protestants.

Catherine: I understand, Sir, but you must also understand that I am a widow, and I simply can't afford such huge fees. I have no choice but to withdraw Hannah from the school.

Headmaster: Withdraw Hannah? But she's our top student!

Catherine: I cannot pay you three times the regular tuition, Sir! That is final.

Headmaster: Very well. We will charge you what we charge the Catholic girls, double the tuition. But please, keep it quiet. Don't advertise this to the other Jews.

(He turns.)

Catherine: Hannah was in love with her school, with her friends, her teachers, and mostly, her poetry. I couldn't take that away from her. She remained enrolled in that school.

Hannah: I was quite well-known in the school for my writing. I began to think, as I got older, that my dream to become a writer like Papa could come true. In the 7th Form, I was especially proud to be elected class representative to the school Literary Society.

8th Form Girl: As President of the Literary Society, I will now call this meeting to order. First, we will see if all new representatives are present. From the 5th Form, Anna Havel? Good. From the 6th Form, Mary? Good. From the

7th Form — wait there must be a mistake . . . Hannah Senesh?

Hannah: Present!

8th Form Girl: Who elected you?

Hannah: My class . . . of course. The 7th Form.

8th Form Girl: I'm sorry, there must have been a misunderstanding. The Literary Society is not for Jewish girls!

Hannah: But I was elected! I love literature, I write . . . I write poetry . . . I —

8th Form Girl: This meeting will be temporarily interrupted until Hannah Senesh removes herself from the premises! The 7th Form will hold new elections and select an appropriate representative.

Hannah: But . . .

8th Form Girl: You are excused, Hannah Senesh! Don't you know what's happening in the world? I wouldn't be so proud to be a Jew!

(8th Form Girl freezes and turns. Hannah alone faces the audience.)

Hannah: Father, if you can hear me, if you are there, please listen! Can you imagine such a thing happening to you — Bela Senesh, barred from the Hungarian Literary Society? I know this is only a girl's school, but I am shocked. Life in Hungary is changing. Where does this hatred and prejudice come from? The whole school knows I should be in the Literary Society. Maybe I should pray, Father. Maybe it is God who can listen to my heart.

(The cast takes the parachute and again circles and sings "Eli, Eli.")

Eli, Eli
Shelo yigamer le'olam
Hachol vehayam
Rishrush shel hamayim
Berak hashamayim
Tefilat ha'adam

My God, my God
I pray that these things never end:
The sand and the sea, the rush of the waters,
The crash of the heavens, the prayer of the heart.

(The ensemble sets the parachute down. Hannah, George, and Catherine come down stage, in the same picture as at the beginning of the play. The radio announcer, stands on one side of the stage.)

Radio Announcer: Good morning, ladies and gentlemen of Hungary. It is March 11, 1938, and important news has been made today. As you know, the Hungarian Parliament has opened debate on what to do about "The Jewish Question." Just as our neighbors in Western Europe are doing, the Hungarians must take precautions to keep these pesky Jews in their proper place. The result of Parliament's debate is the "Jewish Bill," which will reduce the ratio of Jewish representation in the economic field to 20 percent. The Bill states that "the expansion of the Jews is as detrimental to the nation as it is dangerous; we must take steps to defend ourselves against their propagation. Their relegation to the background is a national duty."

Hannah: Background? Why are we dangerous? My father was one of Hungary's greatest playwrights, and he was a Jew!

Catherine: Hannahleh, shhh . . . times are changing now. They will change back soon. It's just some foolishness.

George: What a homecoming! I'm here for a few weeks on school break, only to get news like this. I wish I were back in France. Hungary's not my home any longer.

Catherine: George, you're safer here than in France! I wish you'd consider staying. You could go to university here.

George: Didn't you hear, Mother? They take almost no Jews in the university here.

Catherine: But you are Bela Senesh's son. They will take you!

George: I'm going back to France as soon as I can.

Catherine: This will pass, George. Hungary has always been our home.

Hannah: I think George is right. What kind of home is it, where they turn on you like this?

George: We should have gone with cousin Esther to America. You don't hear such laws passed in their Congress!

Catherine: George, please! Things will be better soon. Please stay. Don't go back to France.

George: I'll get the train schedule. At the end of the week, Mother, I really must leave. There's nothing for me here.

(The Ensemble freezes. Hannah takes a school bag and begins to walk across the stage. Danny and Irma call for her.)

Danny: Hannah, Hannah!

Irma: Hey, Hannah, wait up!

Hannah: Oh, hello.

Danny: Where are you going, Hannah?

Hannah: Just taking a little walk. I want to work on a new poem. I like to sit by the river and write.

Irma: This is no time to be immersed in your poetry, Hannah. Important things are going on in the world.

Hannah: You mean in Germany?

Danny: We mean here. We need to make all the Jewish people aware, there are alternatives to life in the Diaspora.

Irma: Have you heard about the Zionist movement, Hannah?

Hannah: You mean the radicals who actually believe in the writings of Theodor Herzl? They went to live in Palestine. I can't imagine . . .

Danny: Did you listen to the news today, Hannah? Do you think it's safe to stay in Hungary?

Irma: Zionism isn't radical, Hannah, it's real. It's about making a real home, a safe home, for all the Jewish people. Come with us, to a meeting.

Hannah: I told my Mother I would be home early.

Danny: For a little while, Hannah, come.

(They turn upstage and freeze. Eva and Gaby are standing on chairs upstage.)

Eva: To be a Zionist means to be proud to be a Jew!

Gaby: It means to be proud of a two thousand year old history, culture, language — a Jewish peoplehood that Europe is trying to destroy!

Eva: To be a Zionist means to reclaim the Holy Land! All of Europe's Jews should emigrate immediately!

Gaby: To be a Zionist means to revive the Jewish people — so that we are no longer limited to living under European rule. We were once ghettoized here and now our so-called emancipation is quickly leading us back to the ghettos! To be a Zionist means to be free!

Eva: To be a Zionist means we Jews don't want charity or pity! We want a land, we want human rights, we want a Jewish homeland with a Jewish spirit!

Gaby: To be a Zionist means to work long and hard to evacuate Europe's Jews, to find safe routes to travel to Palestine. It means learning to work as agriculturists, as laborers. It means being willing to fight, even die, for what we believe!

Danny: Hannah, what do you think?

Hannah: I don't know what to say. For the first time in my life, I am speechless.

Irma: Will you come back, Hannah? Will you come again to the meeting?

Hannah: Of course I'll come. I, too, am a Zionist!

(Danny and Irma embrace her, then leave. Hannah sits down stage, with Catherine.)

Catherine: It's so quiet here. When Grandma died, the house grew so very quiet. And when George left, it became even more so.

Hannah: I wish he hadn't gone back to France. I don't think it's safe there at all.

Catherine: No, we must convince him to come home to Hungary.

Hannah: Mother, please listen to me. I have something serious, something I've been wanting to talk to you about for weeks. When I go out in the evening with Danny and Irma, we aren't studying . . .

Catherine: Hannaleh, please. I may be your old mother, but I'm a little sharper than you think. I know you're not studying. My goodness you're ready to graduate high school in a few months! I remember my last year, all I did was go on outings with my friends, for ice cream or coffee or . . .

Hannah: Mother! My friends and I don't have that luxury! Not since Germany declared war!

Catherine: Thank goodness we're not in Germany!

Hannah: Mother, in Hungary — every day they pass new laws against the Jews. I wouldn't get accepted to the university — they take so few Jews! I have no future here.

Catherine: Hannah! Did you submit your application yet?

Hannah: Mother, I know this may be hard for you to understand . . . but I want to leave Hungary. I want to go to Palestine. Danny and Irma and I . . . we go to Zionist meetings. There are Jewish people all over Europe, creating ways for other Jews to get safely to the Holy Land.

Catherine: Hannah, what do you know from Palestine? There is nothing there! We are Europeans!

Hannah: No, Mother — first I am a Jew. I believe there must be a homeland, where Jews have human rights, where laws can't be passed that discriminate against us!

Catherine: Hannah, you are so young! The government now — they are just reacting to the world situation. I know it seems bad, but . . .

Hannah: So they take it out on the Jews! No more, Mother. If we have a homeland, we can always be safe. Mother . . . please come with me. Mother dear . . . I couldn't bear to leave you.

Catherine: Hannah, I am an old woman. I can't go traipsing off into the wilderness. Where will you live?

Hannah: I have applied to the Nahalal Girls School. It's an agricultural school, Mother. They teach the girls practical skills, like farming and . . .

Catherine: Hannah, listen to yourself! Farming? What happened to your dream — to be a great writer, like your father?

Hannah: I want to be a writer, but I can't stand by idly while our people are building our homeland. There will be a need for writers later. First, we need farmers. You can't eat books.

Catherine: Hannah, you are my brave girl. You have always been my brave girl.

Hannah: You won't stop me, Mother? You won't stop me from going?

Catherine: *(Laughing.)* Hannah, how could I stop you? You can't stop the ocean . . . you can't stop the crash of the sea . . .

(Hannah and Catherine embrace. Hannah picks up suitcases, and they walk to the "ship." Danny and Irma join them. The Sea Captain stands to the side.)

Sea Captain: Last call! Ship will be leaving port promptly in five minutes! All on board! Ship leaving port in five minutes!

Danny: We will join you soon, Hannah.

Irma: We have more work here, more Jews to convince. Now that Europe is officially at war, it's not so easy to get traveling papers for people. You are lucky to be going now.

Hannah: Mother, do you hear them? Shouldn't you join me now, before it gets too difficult?

Catherine: I will be fine here, my darling. My prayers will be with you, my brave pioneer.

Hannah: I promise to write, as soon as I get there.

Sea Captain: All passengers on board! Raise the gangplank!

(Hannah hugs Danny, Irma, and Catherine. They all say good-bye. Hannah "steps" onto the ship as the three of them back away. Hannah waves slowly.)

Hannah: Good-bye, Europe. Hungary, good-bye!

(After a moment, the Ensemble joins again around the parachute. They circle and sing "Eli, Eli.")

Eli, Eli
Shelo yigamer le'olam
Hachol vehayam
Rishrush shel hamayim
Berak hashamayim
Tefilat ha'adam

My God, my God
I pray that these things never end:
The sand and the sea, the rush of the waters,
The crash of the heavens, the prayer of the heart.

(The ensemble drops the parachute. Hannah comes down stage center. Her family stands behind her, scattered across the stage.)

Hannah: Dear Mother. It's hard to believe that it's already 1940 and I have been in Palestine for over a year. I think I am really succeeding at the Nahalal Girls School! I speak a good deal of Hebrew now. Oh Mother, if you could only see me now — the things I'm learning!

Zionism isn't so romantic. I wash cows every day, I hoe, I do laundry until my fingers are so dry I fear they might fall off! But I am happy, Mother. It is hard to explain — but I feel myself as part of something bigger — of the Jewish people declaring we must survive. I think of Father very often. I hope he would not be disappointed in me. I haven't abandoned my hopes of becoming a writer. When I have a moment, I go off by myself, where no one can find me, and poetry just falls from my heart. I think of you so much, Mother. I know since Grandma's death you must be very lonely. But even of more concern is the situation for the Jews in Europe. Refugees come here to Palestine and tell us horrible things that arc happening in Germany — you can't imagine. I've written George and he, too, feels wholeheartedly sure about Zionism. He is working out a plan to get papers and come here. It could be any day! It is only you, Mother, who is left in Hungary. Please, I beg you — you must come to Palestine! Please Mother, before it is too late . . .

(The Ensemble disperses to the side. Grandma puts on a scarf or hat and becomes Miriam. She embraces Hannah.)

Miriam: Hannah! We did it! I can't believe we're finally graduating. I never thought I'd learn to farm. Back in Europe, I never even saw a hoe! It's strange how your life can change in two years. What's wrong, Hannah? You're not happy?

Hannah: No, I am happy, Miriam. We should be proud.

Miriam: Hannah, you were Nahalal's top student! If anyone should be celebrating, it's you!

Hannah: We all worked hard, Miriam. What's important is that we learned skills to help our country.

Miriam: I know! Next week, a few of us girls are going up north to join a *kibbutz*. What about you, Hannah? Why not join us?

Hannah: I don't know where I want to settle yet. I'm going to travel around *HaAretz* for a while and see what I think.

Miriam: That's just like you, Hannah — you're a poet! You have to explore and wander. Not me! (*Pause.*) You know, I visited that *kibbutz* . . . and it's full of good-looking young boys!

Hannah: I'm not concerned about boys, Miriam. If I find one that's fine . . . if not, that's fine, too.

Miriam: Of course you'll find one! Boys practically throw themselves at your feet!

Hannah: I have more important things on my mind, Miriam. I can't think about boys right now.

Miriam: Hannah, it's your brother — am I right? Oh, I'm so sorry.

Hannah: He was supposed to be here long before now. It's been a full year since he started making plans. What could have gone wrong?

Miriam: I'm sure he'll come, any day.

Hannah: I get no letters from him. All the letters I send get returned.

Miriam: What about your Mother? Has she heard anything?

Hannah: Nothing. And she . . . she still wants to remain in Hungary. It's the only home she knows.

Miriam: Well, Hungary's not under German rule, Hannah.

Hannah: Not yet.

Miriam: What do you mean?

Hannah: I mean that all of Europe is in danger. It's 1941 and Germany hasn't been stopped. I have to do something. I can't just stand here idle and helpless.

Miriam: Hannah, you are doing something. We all are. You're here in Palestine, building a homeland for the Jews. This is the most important thing you can do.

Hannah: Miriam, you're not thinking about the main problem! How will Jews get here? What's the use of building a homeland if none of the Jews from Europe can get to it? Where is my brother? Why hasn't he been able to come?

Miriam: (*Quietly.*) I don't know, Hannah.

Hannah: I don't know what I'm going to do, Miriam. But I will do something.

Miriam: You have always been different from the rest of us, Hannah. I don't understand you. But I love you. Good luck.

Hannah: Good luck on the *kibbutz*, Miriam. I will come visit you!

(They embrace and Miriam goes off to the side. Hannah again moves down stage and Catherine stands just behind her, to the side.)

Hannah: Dear Mother. I am so saddened. It is now 1943 and I have heard nothing from George! Each day I wake up with hope for his arrival, but by evening I am so saddened, it is hard to sleep. Please, Mother — speak to the Zionists in Budapest, you really must come here! I am enjoying life on the *kibbutz*, here at Sdot Yam, but I feel frustrated that I can't do more to help the Jews of Europe. I have been recommended for enlistment in the army. I know that may shock you, but here in Palestine, girls are fighting. Every person needs to help. It is really a great thing to be a girl and have every chance to help your country! But what I really want to do is figure out some way I could return to Hungary in order to help the Jews there emigrate. If only there was a way . . .

(Catherine moves to the side and Ari enters.)

Hannah: Hello, can I help you? Have you been to our *kibbutz* before?

Ari: No, no I haven't. I'm looking for a Hannah Senesh.

Hannah: That's me.

Ari: Ari Katz. *(They shake hands.)* I am officer in the Haganah. I understand you're interested in enlistment?

Hannah: Yes, I've been thinking about it. I think I would be a good soldier.

Ari: You have excellent references from the people at the Nahalal Girls School and from this *kibbutz*. They say there's no harder worker, no more outspoken opinionated girl.

Hannah: That's not fair, I just . . .

Ari: It's all right, Hannah. We need someone like you for a special mission. Someone unusually brave, determined, maybe a little crazy. This mission is top secret.

Hannah: Why me? What's the mission?

Ari: You grew up in Hungary, right?

Hannah: Yes, I lived there all my life until I came to *HaAretz*.

Ari: And you are very concerned? You want to help the Jews in Hungary? You are willing to do that in any way possible?

Hannah: Yes, absolutely!

Ari: You will jump out of a plane?

Hannah: Jump? Out of a plane?

Ari: That is required.

Hannah: Then, yes, I can jump out of a plane.

Ari: This will be a secret mission. You are the only woman selected to go. We are working under the auspices of the British Army. You will become a British officer. To get into Hungary, we must parachute into Yugoslavia. The Partisans there will lead us across the border. If we make it, we will round up as many Jews as possible and lead them back to Palestine.

Hannah: I don't know how . . . to jump out of a plane.

Ari: (*Laughing.*) Don't worry, Hannah. You'll have plenty of training. All of the selected soldiers will first go to Cairo to practice parachuting skills. You need to pack some things, Hannah. You'll be leaving soon.

Hannah: But, I can't leave now. I'm waiting . . . you see, my brother George is to arrive any day, and . . .

Ari: Where is he coming from?

Hannah: France.

Ari: I wouldn't count on his arrival, Hannah. This mission can't wait.

Hannah: But he'll be here any day. I haven't seen him in years. He went to study in France when I was still in high school, and —

Ari: If you choose to join our mission, come to this address in one week. *(He hands her a slip of paper.)* Don't tell anyone what our mission is — only that you're enlisting in the British army. I hope you won't disappoint me, Hannah.

(He exits.)

Hannah: But George?

(Hannah comes down stage.)

Hannah: Dear God. Tomorrow I leave Palestine to go to Cairo. I know I must join this mission, I have no other choice. I must help the Jews of Hungary. Every morning, I come to this seaport and wait. Ships arrive. Passengers get off the ship. Some of them can barely walk. They haven't eaten for days, maybe weeks. They are so weak. George is never among them. I look at every face. What if one of them is George, but I just don't recognize him? Am I the same Hannah? Would he recognize me?

(Sound of ship's arrival. Hannah stands, as if looking at the passengers. George enters.)

George: Hannah? Hannah — is it you?

Hannah: George? George?

George: My Hannah! Come here!

(They embrace and are silent for a moment.)

Hannah: George, this is a miracle! I don't know what to say . . .

George: I knew you wouldn't give up on me. You gave me hope. You knew I'd make it.

Hannah: George, you're so thin. Let's go get you some food, new clothes, and a hot bath.

George: I'm fine, Hannah. Now that I've seen you.

Hannah: You must tell me your story — everything that's happened since I saw you last.

George: In time, Hannah. In time.

Hannah: George, you don't understand what a miracle this is. I'm leaving tomorrow. I'm enlisting in the British army. I'm going on a secret mission. I can't tell you what it is. But it's a wonderful thing, George, a wonderful thing.

George: That's my Hannah! You haven't changed a bit. You were always the strongest, most determined little girl — so full of faith and courage. Now you are a woman. You've become a beautiful woman, Hannah. God has answered my prayers. Only to see you — so young and beautiful and brave.

Hannah: George, I will take you to my *kibbutz*, where everyone will help you and take care of you. You will love Palestine, George. Oh, I can't bear it! We have so much to say and there is only one day.

George: We'll make the most of it, Hannah. And when you return from your secret mission, then we will really celebrate. (*Pause.*) Aren't you scared at all? Must you really go?

Hannah: Don't worry about me. I'll be fine. (*Pause.*) I'll tell you one thing you just won't believe. George, I'm going to jump out of a plane!

(George joins the Ensemble. They grab the parachute and lift it. Hannah stands under it in the middle of the stage. She spins slowly in a circle and she sings "Eli, Eli.")

Eli, Eli
Shelo yigamer le'olam
Hachol vehayam
Rishrush shel hamayim
Berak hashamayim
Tefilat ha'adam

My God, my God
I pray that these things never end:

The sand and the sea, the rush of the waters,
The crash of the heavens, the prayer of the heart.

(Hannah steps down stage and stands absolutely still. The Ensemble moves to the side of the stage. Guard approaches Hannah.)

Guard: You will give us the information . . . now.

Hannah: I will never tell you. Nothing.

Guard: Perhaps, another beating? Or maybe we shouldn't feed you? How about that?

Hannah: I will not give any information to the Hungarian government or to the Gestapo. Never.

Guard: I think I can change your mind. We have brought someone to see you. Another prisoner. Maybe after you see her, you will talk.

(Guard brings Catherine face to face with Hannah.)

Guard: I will give you two a few moments alone. To talk.

(He exits.)

Hannah: Forgive me, Mother. Please forgive me.

Catherine: Hannah? Hannah?

Hannah: Mother? Oh, what have they done to you?

Catherine: I'm fine, Hannah. They treat me very well. I haven't been here long. But look at you. Hannah, your face is bruised. Your hair hasn't been washed. Oh, my darling.

Hannah: Mother, don't worry about me. I am strong. I never thought they would touch you. I never thought all this mess . . . would affect you.

Catherine: Hannah, why aren't you in Palestine? Safe with George?

Hannah: I can't explain it, Mother. They are probably listening. I left Palestine to come to Hungary to save the Jews here. I didn't think I'd be captured. I am a British Officer.

Catherine: Please, Hannah, tell me you didn't do this — to save me?

Hannah: It wasn't just you, Mother. I learned about the horrors that were happening to the Jews in Europe. I couldn't be happy without trying to help. That's all there is to it.

Catherine: Oh, my brave girl. What now, Hannah? They won't let you go unless you tell them all of this.

Hannah: I can't betray my mission, Mother. There are others here, who are succeeding.

Catherine: But what will happen to you, Hannah?

Hannah: Don't worry, Mother. They're scared of me — all the guards, the officers! They've never met a girl like me!

Catherine: You are my Hannah. I love you, darling.

Hannah: Mother, I love you.

Guard: *(Entering.)* That's enough conversation, Mrs. Senesh. You will be escorted back to your cell. I'm sure Hannah will have a lot to talk about now.

(He pulls Hannah out. He moves her so she is standing upstage, with her back to the audience. He moves to the side.)

Catherine: My Hannah never told the Hungarians or the Germans the information they wanted. She remained in solitary confinement. She was routinely beaten and starved. I was held in prison for a time, and Hannah and I found ways to communicate. Most of the female guards would help us — they loved my Hannah. She would often tell me, see, Mother, I have a mission here in prison, I'm making everyone a Zionist!

(The members of the family, except Hannah, all join Catherine, posing in the original family snapshot that opened the show. They do not smile.)

Sometimes I look at our old family portraits. My husband would never have believed that such disgrace could befall his beloved Hungary. I am grateful to God that my Mother died before witnessing such atrocities. And I am grateful that my son George lived and that I could join him in Palestine, where Hannah always wanted me to go. As for my Hannah? On November 7, 1944, Hannah was executed in prison. She was buried in the Jewish Cemetery in Budapest in the Martyr's section. You can see her grave there. We can't imagine how such a miracle occurred. Such a miracle was unthinkable in those days.

(Hannah walks down stage and joins her family.)

Hannah: Don't be deterred. Don't be afraid. We all must struggle. Until there is liberty for all. Liberty for all.

(Hannah and the Ensemble softly hum "Eli Eli." They exit.)

Hannah Senesh, *poet and fighter, trained under the British in Cairo in parachuting, infiltration, sabotage, and espionage techniques. She was parachuted into Yugoslavia near the Hungarian border. She was captured with a radio transmitter and imprisoned. After a long and brutal imprisonment, during which she did not surrender any useful military information, Senesh was killed by a Nazi firing squad. She was 23 years old. In 1950, her remains were brought to Haifa for a burial in a military cemetery with full military honors. Senesh's diary, which included her poetry, was published after her death, and has enjoyed wide popularity throughout the world. Her brief poems are very moving and poignant. Some have been made into songs; one has been included in a Haggadah. She serves as a model of courage and bravery.*

www.ingramcontent.com/pod-product-compliance
Lightning Source LLC
Jackson TN
JSHW011936131224
75386JS00041B/1415